A NEW BEGINNING:

RECASTING THE U.S.–JAPAN ECONOMIC RELATIONSHIP

Bruce Stokes

A Council on Foreign Relations Paper

CONTENTS

FOREWORD

Unfortunately, Japan has almost slipped from the U.S. radar screen. Flush with a self-confidence born of recent economic success and preoccupied with China, Washington has largely ignored its relationship with the world's second-largest economy.

Japan has stagnated economically for a decade, forcing the United States to carry much of the burden of world economic growth. Japan's unprecedented government debt, its lingering banking problems, and its unfunded insurance and pension obligations remain a dark cloud on the financial horizon. The U.S. trade deficit with Japan continues to grow—a worrisome potential political problem for both countries.

Yet there is reason for hope. The long-awaited Japanese economic recovery may be at hand. Economic restructuring has begun. Foreign investment is on the rise.

With new governments soon to be in place in both Washington and Tokyo, it is time for an ambitious new beginning for the U.S.-Japan economic relationship: a joint commitment to create an "open marketplace" by the year 2010.

This positive vision must be backed by a new tough-mindedness in Washington toward Japan, both to defend America's growing business interests in a resurgent Japanese economy and to encourage Tokyo to seize the opportunity afforded by the advent of new governments and the revival of hope for Japan's economic future.

With the ever-present cost of continuing to ignore the problem set in an environment of change and opportunity, the Council on Foreign Relations assembled a group of America's leading experts on Japan—including members from academe, Wall Street, Capitol Hill, and former government officials—to help us think through a recasting of the U.S.-Japan economic relationship.

This group, chaired by Senator Jay Rockefeller (D–W.Va.) and Representative Amo Houghton (R–N.Y.) sought to develop a two-pronged U.S. economic strategy toward Japan that would both assert U.S. economic interests and reinvigorate U.S. economic ties with Japan. This paper by Council Senior Fellow Bruce Stokes is based on those deliberations.

Lawrence J. Korb
Maurice R. Greenberg Chair, Director of Studies
Council on Foreign Relations

ACKNOWLEDGMENTS

Senator Jay Rockefeller (D–W.Va.) and Representative Amo Houghton (R–N.Y.), co-chairs of the study group that served as the resource and the sounding board for this paper, are all America could ever ask for in public servants. For many years, they have both been deeply involved in U.S.-Japan relations, in both the public and the private sectors. In recent years, when Japan faded from America's radar screen, they have been lonely voices urging Washington to refocus the U.S. relationship with the world's second-largest economy. At times tough-minded critics of Japan, they both have the statesman's sense to look beyond the immediate trade battles to chart a new, more positive course for the relationship. I have immense admiration for them both and will forever be deeply in their debt.

The members of the study group have my special thanks. They contributed background papers to this project. They read and commented on drafts of this paper. Most important, they contributed their time and their insights during numerous study group sessions. Members of the study group often disagreed but did so respectfully. Many were good friends before this process began. More are deep friends now.

All projects of this magnitude require financial angels, and the Council was blessed with two: the Japan-U.S. Friendship Commission and the U.S.-Japan Foundation. Their support was invaluable. More important, Eric J. Gangloff, the executive director of the Friendship Commission, and George Packard, president of the U.S.-Japan Foundation, enthusiastically embraced this paper from the beginning, lending their insight, their experience, and above all, their friendship throughout the process.

Leslie H. Gelb, the Council's president, Gary C. Hufbauer, the Council's former vice president and director of Studies, and Lawrence J. Korb, the current vice president and director of Studies, supported this project from its inception. The Council provides a unique environment where intellectuals and practitioners can work together. No author could have a better home in which to develop policy-relevant analyses and recommendations.

The Pacific Council on International Policy hosted study group sessions in Los Angeles, San Francisco, and Seattle. Kenneth H. Keller, the Council's former senior vice president for Programs and acting director of Studies, hosted a session in Minneapolis, and Glen S. Fukushima, vice chair of the Board of Directors at the Japan-U.S. Friendship Commission and president and representative director of Arthur D. Little (Japan), Inc., hosted a session in Tokyo. Each meeting contributed substantively to this study, allowing me to test out policy recommendations on individuals with real world experience in dealing with Japan.

I am immeasurably indebted to Council research associates Eric Drabiuk, Olivia Rivera, and Jessica Duda, each of whom spent many hours organizing study group sessions, writing up meeting minutes, and tracking countless details. They are the Council's unsung heroes.

Tamera Luzzatto, Senator Rockefeller's chief of staff, and Bob Van Wicklin, Representative Houghton's legislative director, went out of their way to help mesh busy legislative schedules with the demands of the study group.

Patricia Lee Dorff, the Council's director of publishing, and other members of Council publisher David Kellogg's editorial team provided invaluable advice, prodding, and counsel. Never have so few done so much for such undeserving authors.

In the end, the sole responsibility for this paper lies with the author. The analysis and recommendations expressed here do not necessarily reflect the views of any of the study group participants or of my co-chairs.

A New Beginning:
Recasting the U.S.-Japan
Economic Relationship

Bruce Stokes

EXECUTIVE SUMMARY

The time is ripe for a bold new initiative to recast the U.S.-Japan economic partnership for the 21st century. A new Japan is emerging. Foreign investment is on the rise. Tokyo is deregulating and restructuring its economy. A new generation of Japanese entrepreneurs and venture capitalists has arrived on the stage.

But a more vibrant, sustainable Japanese economy is not foreordained. It has a limited time to take root before the crushing weight of Japan's mounting public debt, the burden of its aging and shrinking population, and the cumulative toll of years of economic stagnation could cripple the world's second-largest economy and America's principal economic and security partner in Asia.

New governments in Washington and Tokyo must seize this moment. To reinvigorate the U.S.-Japan relationship and to accelerate the pace and redirect the nature of change in the Japanese economy, the next American president should challenge his Japanese counterpart to create a U.S.-Japan "open marketplace"—one free of tariffs and with minimal regulatory impediments and an increasing freedom to do business—by the year 2010.

For such an ambitious initiative to be successful, Tokyo must finally break with the past and transform itself from an industrial to an information economy, shift its perspective from domestic to global, and abandon its failing efforts to preserve its place in the twentieth century industrial economy to carve out a new role for Japan in the 21st–century information economy. Washington, for its part, must be willing to take the risks inherent in embracing greater economic integration with Tokyo. And it must be willing to pursue a tough-minded approach to bilateral economic issues if and when Japan's restructuring resolve falters.

Recasting the U.S.-Japan economic relationship is particularly challenging because the Japanese economy is a profound enigma. There is no doubt that Japan is in economic transition. But the pace and nature of that change is uncertain. Economic restructuring that does not address the concerns of Japan's global economic partners may be tumultuous in the context of Japanese society yet insufficient for the needs of the world economy. Japan still remains less open to foreign manufacturers and foreign investors than any other major industrial society. The Japanese economy continues to underperform, faring worse for longer than any other major industrial power in the last half century. Japanese government debt, which now exceeds the value of the economy, threatens to spiral out of control unless economic growth picks up. And since Japan has the oldest population in the industrial world, the cost of supporting its aging citizens will begin draining it of savings by the end of the decade.

The United States has a tremendous stake in the resolution of Japan's economic problems. American exporters can ill afford the world's second-largest market to remain relatively closed. Those who have invested in Japan in recent years should not have the fruits of their efforts limited by Japan's domestic market failures. American home buyers should not have to pay higher mortgage rates because of the Japanese government's burgeoning borrowing needs. And the United States should not continue to bear the lion's share of the Asian defense burden because of Japan's economic shortcomings.

The immediate danger for the United States is that Japan will muddle through its current economic crisis, fiddle around the edges of its economic structure, fix only what has to be fixed, and restore some modicum of growth without ever really changing the core of its economic system. This would be a prescription for slow growth, marginal integration with the global economy, and even greater problems in future bilateral economic relations.

A new, proactive U.S. economic policy toward Japan is needed to avoid such an outcome. To be successful, that policy must necessarily be two-pronged: short-term and long-term, macroeconomic and microeconomic, systemic and sector-specific, practical and visionary, and supportive and challenging—in other words, it should offer both carrots and sticks.

The cornerstone of a new American economic posture toward Japan is the creation of a U.S.-Japan "open marketplace" by 2010. Washington and Tokyo should commit themselves to creating an open marketplace—free of tariffs, with minimal regulatory impediments, and with increasing freedom to do business. Such an initiative would encompass further Japanese deregulation, the enforcement of competition laws, the facilitation of foreign investment, and a greater importation of manufactured products. It would necessarily be reciprocal, requiring changes in U.S. restrictions on government procurement and foreign investment.

To further that goal a new U.S. administration should press the Japanese government to do the following things:

- *Restore economic growth.* Experience over the last decade demonstrates that if enough money is pumped into the Japanese economy, expansion will follow. Fiscal stimulus is obviously a fool's errand if it is merely a substitute for structural reform. But in the short run, priming the pump remains indispensable to avoiding a recurrence of recession. New spending should be refocused on urban and information infrastructures and in selected tax cuts.

- *Accelerate restructuring.* Restructuring has begun, but it has a long way to go. By any measure—the reduction in excess capacity, unemployment, bankruptcies, and mergers and acquisitions—Japan has yet to experience the kind of restructuring other recession-plagued industrial nations have gone through in the past. It must become easier for the Japanese to get out of businesses, create new enterprises and jobs, and shift from job to job.

- *Expedite deregulation.* Deregulation of the Japanese marketplace—especially in key sectors such as telecommunications, transportation, and electricity—would do more to spur Japan's economic recovery, open the Japanese economy to foreign competition, and improve U.S.-Japan economic relations than would any other single initiative.

- *Strengthen competition policy.* The cartelized nature of much of the Japanese marketplace aggravates U.S.-Japan trade problems, such as in the steel industry, and denies American firms the full benefits of their recent investments there. To leverage better Japanese enforcement of its own antitrust laws, the United States should file antitrust cases against practices that exclude American firms from the Japanese market.

- *Reform corporate governance.* Corporate governance reform—including bringing in outside boards of directors and adopting "global best practice" accounting methods—will force Japanese firms to focus more intently on returns on equity, which in turn will undermine import-restricting exclusionary business practices, make it easier for foreigners to acquire local sales and service firms, and inhibit Japanese firms' predatory export pricing by making the expansion of productive capacity more sensitive to the true cost of capital.

- *Encourage foreign direct investment.* The current flood of foreign investors is transforming Japan's sheltered domestic corporate environment much as Commodore Matthew Perry's black ships transformed Japanese society more than a century ago. This wave of mergers and acquisitions can only be sustained if Japan continues to deregulate, restructure, and create a more competitive economy.

To support a renewed focus on Japan, the new U.S. administration should:

- *Pursue a proactive trade policy.* Years of trade jousting with Japan has taught valuable lessons: success requires leverage; it pays to have specific demands; short time frames lead to truncated results; and fragmentation within the U.S. government has frequently been Japan's most powerful ally. The new U.S. administration should be willing to use all available trade tools in dealing with Japan, including new structural and sectoral initiatives, stepped-up unilateral trade action, and multilateral pressure through cases before the World Trade Organization (WTO). It must invest the resources to create a Japan team in the U.S. government capable of supporting a new Japan policy. And Congress should reassert its constitutional role in trade policy, if only to prod the administration to adopt a more assertive policy toward Japan.

- *Not shy away from gaiatsu.* Washington's pressure on Tokyo for change must not be deterred by Tokyo's resistance. But America should learn to talk softly and carry a big stick.

- *Launch a political dialogue.* A more democratic Japanese political system is a necessary precursor to a more market-oriented Japanese economy. The U.S.-Japan economic dialogue must be broadened to include frank discussion with a cross section of the Japanese society about the political impediments to Japan's economic renewal.

In the end, Washington should never forget that solutions to many of its Japan problems start at home. The most important things the United States can do to prepare itself for the ups and downs in bilateral relations rest solely in its hands. To contend with the Japan challenge, American companies must remain at the technological cutting edge, and America's educational system and its workforce must continue to improve. The nation must save more and spend the federal budget surplus wisely if it is to contain the trade deficit.

In a feel-good era when the American economy is enjoying unprecedented success, when Americans are captivated with China and tired of Japan, the status quo toward Japan is the path of least resistance. But such passivity in the face of the staggering economic problems facing the world's second-largest economy and America's principal Asian ally would be a profound mistake. Charting a new course for the U.S.-Japan economic relationship will require American assertiveness and a bold vision for a better future. It is a legacy for the new U.S. administration, a new Congress, and a new Japanese government—if they all have the courage to begin writing it today.

A NEW BEGINNING

At the beginning of a new millennium, on the eve of a new American presidency, with a new U.S. Congress in the offing, and with a new Japanese government in place, the time is ripe for a bold new initiative to recast the U.S.-Japan economic partnership for the 21st century. For too long, the U.S.-Japan business and commercial relationship has been a troubled one. In the 1980s, tension grew out of American frustration with the closed nature of the Japanese economy and fear of both the bilateral trade imbalance and Japan's economic ascendance. In the 1990s, conversely, the source of bilateral unease was Japan's fear of America's economic revival and its own precariously weak economy. Another decade of tensions, troubles, and drift in the relationship is in the offing, thanks to Japan's economic stagnation, the rising U.S. trade deficit with Japan and ongoing U.S. market access problems in Japan, growing U.S. frustration with Japan's avoidance of the burden of global economic leadership, and the impending global economic problems attendant upon Japan's rising deficit and rapidly aging population. A different script for the future is therefore in the interests of Japan, the United States, and the world.

A new Japan is struggling to rise out of the ashes of the old one. Foreign investment is on the rise in Japan. Tokyo is deregulating and restructuring its economy. A new generation of entrepreneurs and venture capitalists has emerged. And the Japanese economy shows signs of a halting recovery. These economic changes and the accompanying political ones are historically unprecedented, may be irreversible, and are largely underestimated in the United States. The opportunity exists to take advantage of this process of change to chart a new direction for the U.S.-Japan relationship.

New governments in Washington and Tokyo must seize this moment. Japan's commitment to economic liberalization is tenuous at best and must be locked in before reactionary forces stifle reform. And U.S. willingness to deal creatively with Japan is dangerously dependent on its own continued economic good fortune and could turn sour in an economic downturn.

To reinvigorate ties and maximize the benefits that Japan and the United States could derive from their economic interaction, Washington should challenge Tokyo to complete its economic liberalization and restructuring in the context of a joint commitment to creating a U.S.-Japan open marketplace—free of tariffs, with minimal regulatory impediments and an increasing freedom to do business—by the year 2010. Future U.S. economic policy toward Japan—be it quiet diplomacy, joint initiatives, decisions about the exchange rate, bilateral and multilateral trade actions, or congressional trade oversight—should be geared to that end.

Such an effort will be an uphill struggle. Garnering U.S. public support will require tangible evidence that Japan continues to open its economy to the rest of the world. To sustain the business community's support, a balanced handling of both market access concerns and the new problems confronting Americans now doing business in Japan must occur. It will demand the artful application of U.S. pressure—diplomatic and trade policy *jujitsu* to maintain momentum and demonstrate the seriousness of American purpose. It will require a judicious balancing of carrot and stick approaches and a willingness to be tough whenever strategically necessary, coupled with diplomatic sensitivity in choosing one's battles. At the same time, a new Japan policy must avoid the application of blunt force that increasingly evokes Japanese resistance. And it must be reciprocal. A shared open marketplace will require regulatory and market adaptation on both sides of the Pacific—including the mutual recognition of regulatory standards and changes in U.S. public procurement practices—because interdependence is a two-way street.

However, a renewed American focus on U.S.-Japan economic relations and new Washington policy initiatives toward Tokyo outside the context of a broader effort at market integration would simply be a prescription for a new round of trade tensions. Setting an ambitious bilateral economic goal without concrete benchmarks along the way and without a willingness to see that they are achieved would be a recipe for failure, and more important, it would ignore America's vital national interest in Japan's speedy economic recovery. Only by embedding individual trade and investment problems and concerns about the structure of the Japanese economy within the context of a decade-long, comprehensive effort to craft an open marketplace can Washington and Tokyo jointly chart a new course for their economic relations.

To be successful, such an initiative will require political risk-taking on both sides of the Pacific. Tokyo must be willing to accelerate its current pace of change and lock in reforms. Washington must embrace economic integration with Japan and overcome Japan's reluctance to open up to the world through a tough-minded American approach to bilateral economic issues.

The task is daunting. Trust is lacking on both sides of the Pacific. Japan's track record on liberalization is far from perfect. America's notoriously short attention span and its proclivity to lecture its trading partners are impediments to any long-term cooperative initiative. But the stakes are high. And no less ambition should be expected of the relationship between the world's two largest economies.

A RELATIONSHIP OUT OF FOCUS

Japan has incongruously slipped from America's national radar screen. The U.S. trade deficit with Japan reached a new record in 1999, yet there was no clamoring from the business community or on Capitol Hill to do something about this imbalance, unlike during much of the 1980s when the U.S. deficit with Japan was smaller. In 1998, Japan's recession, sliding stock market, and burgeoning financial sector debt caused widespread anxiety that it would pull the world into a depression. When no disaster ensued, Japan's ongoing economic woes disappeared from the front pages of American newspapers and out of the consciousness of American political and business leaders. A decade ago, Americans were convinced that Japanese companies could out-compete their U.S. counterparts and would soon dominate the world. Then, because the weakness of domestically oriented Japanese firms had been exposed, the continued international competitiveness of globally minded Japanese corporations was largely ignored. Even among America's Japan experts, business leaders with investments in Japan, and politicians traditionally concerned with the bilateral relationship, there was an ennui born of frustration and disillusionment with Japan's failure to change substantively within a meaningful time frame.

The U.S.-Japan relationship has long been typified by prolonged indifference punctuated by sharp bouts of economic friction. History and an array of festering problems suggest that American apathy toward Japan could turn to anger once again. This newfound focus of attention would undoubtedly evoke Japanese resentment and recrimination. It is a potent prescription for renewed bilateral economic friction that could easily pollute the security and diplomatic relationship.

Washington's possible refocus on Tokyo will be driven by a conjunction of factors. For the first time in recent history, American companies and investors have established a beachhead "inside the castle" of the Japanese economy, thanks to high-profile investments in the financial sector, the auto industry, and the equities market. This positioning poses a host of potential new bilateral points of friction involving the implementation of domestic competition policy, tax and regulatory matters, transparency in government decision-making, and so forth. Although these investment-related matters may, in the long term, be tangentially part of the government-to-government dialogue over market access, their purely domestic aspect is rapidly moving to the center of the bilateral relationship.

The inevitable resumption of Japan's aborted economic recovery will only heighten, rather than reduce, many bilateral trade tensions. Once the Japanese economy has been removed from Washington's critical list, prior inhibitions about more insistently pressing Tokyo for reform will melt away.

The overall U.S. trade imbalance and the U.S. trade deficit with Japan are both in record territory. A U.S. economic slowdown with attendant rising unemployment and the likely use of Japan as a scapegoat may be unavoidable during the tenure of the next American president. Any slowdown in U.S. domestic demand will raise the premium on sustaining U.S. exports, highlighting persistent market-access problems in Japan, and maximizing the benefits of recent U.S. investments in Japan.

At the same time, it is increasingly obvious how dangerously dependent the world economy is on the single engine of American economic expansion. Japan's periodic flirtations with recession are a stark reminder of the ever-present threat that a weak Japan poses to global economic well-being.

Japan's annual government deficit and overall public debt are growing threats to global capital markets. So far, the Japanese government's need for capital has largely been satisfied by its preferred access to domestic Japanese savings. Ongoing financial liberalization in Japan will increase competition for that capital, raising the government's borrowing costs and, potentially, the cost of money around the world—especially if Japanese public indebtedness continues to expand.

Finally, Japan's backsliding on reform is now obvious. Years of frustrated reform initiatives in Tokyo demonstrate the difficulty

Japan's government, business sector, and society at large have in staying the course of economic restructuring on their own. In 2000, domestic opposition to restructuring the Japanese economy was increasingly apparent. An anti-reform caucus in the Japanese legislature, the Diet, included as members more than half the ruling Liberal Democratic Party (LDP). Accounting reforms, once touted as a means of giving capital markets a true picture of Japanese companies' financial situations, and bank deposit reimbursement limits, intended to make consumers more responsible and banks more responsive, were postponed until after the 2000 election. As economic recovery picks up steam, backsliding on reform could accelerate.

AN ECONOMIC ENIGMA

Recasting the U.S.-Japan economic relationship is a particular challenge because the Japanese economy is a profound enigma. The new Japan is having trouble setting down firm roots. Japanese economic reforms are much more impressive when measured against traditional Japanese practices than they are when compared with 21st-century global standards. And the case for Washington to refocus on the bilateral relationship is perversely undermined by the fact that Japan's continued failure to lift itself out of its economic doldrums has yet to pose any real threat to America or to the global economy.

In early 1999, Japan showed signs of its old dynamism. Economic growth was on the upswing. Dynamic start-up companies fueled a stock market recovery. The information sector of the economy was growing at the phenomenal rate of 12 percent per year.[1] Corporate profits were rising—a precondition for self-sustained recovery. Cross shareholding and the *keiretsu* business relationships that typified the old closed nature of the Japanese economy were eroding. Major banks had been allowed to fail, sparking heretofore unimaginable consolidations among financial institutions. For the first time, foreigners were permitted to acquire controlling interests in securities firms, banks, and major manufacturers. International investors responded in a rush. Deregulation was a government mantra. A new business mentality—demonstrated by unprecedented risk-taking, promises of new labor-market flexibility, and surprising attention to shareholder value—began to emerge.

At the same time, this new Japan drew sustenance from the old economy's inherent strengths. With its high savings rate and the world's largest current account surplus, the nation remained the world's principal source of capital. Discerning consumers continued to demand that Japanese companies operate at the cutting edge.

---

[1] Andrew Shipley, Schroders Japan, private communication, December 15, 1999.

And a well-trained workforce enabled Japanese manufacturers to do so. A continuing trade surplus was the tangible manifestation of the competitiveness of major Japanese multinational firms.

But the budding signs of an economic spring were dashed, at least temporarily, when the Japanese economy shrank in the last half of 1999, marking the return of recession. This contraction was due largely to cutbacks in public expenditures, compounded by heightened job insecurity and wage cuts that made Japanese consumers wary of new spending. But the downturn also reflected the fact that banks, insurance companies, and pension funds remain buried under staggering mountains of bad debts and unfunded liabilities. And Tokyo's commitment to fundamental deregulation had stagnated.

This economic reversal reopened the debate over whether Japan was recovering or relapsing, over whether Tokyo was reforming or retrenching. It highlighted a broader dilemma in assessing the state of the Japanese economy. It is irrefutable that the nature and structure of Japan's business environment is changing in profound ways. Yet, what is the correct point of comparison? Recovery and reform are both relative concepts. Change can only be judged by the benchmark against which it is set. Compared with Japan's past, the country has made great strides, even in the last few years. But in a rapidly evolving world, that is the wrong criterion. In a competitive global marketplace, the goal posts are constantly changing. Japan should not be judged by where it has come from but by where it is going and how it measures up to its competitors in that race. Assessing the nation's progress toward a new Japan using a global standard, not comparing it with the old Japan, the nation has a long way to go.

The Japanese economy has performed worse for longer than any other major industrial power has in the last half century. Japan still remains less open to foreign manufacturers and foreign investors than is any other major industrial society. At a time when governments in both Europe and the United States have finally gotten their budget deficits under control, the size of the Japan's budget deficit and its total debt raise questions about the country's sustainability. Many small and medium-sized domestically

oriented Japanese firms are woefully uncompetitive internationally. Corporate mergers and acquisitions, although on the rise, are
still a fraction of those in the United Kingdom or the United States.
Japan's unemployment rate remains half that of comparable recession-plagued economies of the past, suggesting a deep-seated
unwillingness to suffer through the necessary structural adjustments
endured by every other industrial economy that has attempted to
make the transition to the information age.

The danger for the United States is that Japan will muddle through
its current economic crisis, fiddle around the edges of the structure of the economy, fix only what has to be fixed, and restore some
modicum of growth without ever really changing the core of its
economic system.

This is unacceptable. Another decade of slow growth in Japan
is a recipe for trouble for both the island nation and for the world.
The Japanese population will begin to decline by 2008. The workforce is already shrinking. As a result, the number of people
working to support the old and the young is steadily declining. Without significant structural economic reform that spurs a rapid
return to sustainable economic growth, Japan's ability to sustain
its aging population will be severely impaired, placing ever greater
pressure on its public finances.

There is no doubt that Japan is in transition—economically, politically, and culturally. But psychologists sometimes joke that individuals never change but just become more like themselves. Does
the same hold true for societies? Are the changes Japan is now experiencing leading to the creation of a new, more open, more globally minded Japan, as the United States fervently hopes? Or is Japan
merely transforming itself into a 21st-century version of the old
Japan, one that is certainly more integrated into the international economy but still largely operates on its own terms and only min-
imally accommodates the needs of the world?

The challenge facing the United States in dealing with this changing Japan—be it on broad fiscal and monetary policy issues or on
narrow trade, competition policy, and regulatory concerns—is
the pace and nature of that change. Change outside a relevant time
frame is noteworthy only to historians. Change that does not address

the concerns of Japan's global economic partners may be tumultuous in the context of Japanese society yet insufficient for world economic needs.

For example, Japan's willingness to accept greater foreign investment has created tremendous opportunities for American companies to leap over long-standing trade barriers and become major players in the Japanese domestic market. But Washington should entertain no false illusions about the purchase of the Long-Term Credit Bank by Ripplewood Holdings or Daimler-Chrysler's buying of a stake in Mitsubishi Motors Corporation. Japan is engaged in a forced sale of depressed assets. The true test of Tokyo's embrace of deeper integration with the global economy will be whether foreign investors are able to nurture these crippled companies back to health and, in the process, expand their market share and diversify their holdings. Such an evolution will require true national treatment of foreign investors—a profound step for Japan.

Similarly, Washington has long assumed that pressuring Tokyo to jump-start the Japanese economy through government spending will in turn dramatically boost Japan's import performance, helping reignite Asian economic growth while easing the U.S.-Japan trade imbalance. But the trickle-down effect of Japanese recovery will be limited without further deregulation and a restructuring of the Japanese economy. Before its current crisis, Japan imported fewer manufactured products as a portion of its economy than any other industrial nation. The simple resumption of growth will not change Japan's low proclivity to import. Only structural reform will.

Of course, even a cursory knowledge of Japanese society suggests that Tokyo will never be able to achieve all the reforms Washington and the rest of the world expect of it. Japan will never become, nor should it necessarily aspire to be, the perfect model of an Anglo-Saxon market economy. Therefore, U.S. policy toward Japan must be designed to accommodate the unavoidable tension between what Japan can do (from the Japanese point of view) and what Japan must do (from the world's point of view).

Finally, Japan's haltingly slow recovery is a deeply troubling performance by the world's second-largest economy. It places the burden of sustaining global economic growth on the United States, Europe, and others. The failure to clean up both the books in Japan's financial sector and the rising government indebtedness is a source of potential instability in global capital markets. The fragile Japanese economy remains susceptible to even minor economic shocks that could reverberate around the world. The cartel-like nature of major Japanese industrial sectors sustain production over capacity, leading to dumping abroad and charges of unfair competition in export markets. And Japan's continued economic weakness and growing debt erode its ability to contribute to the security and economic development of East Asia.

Yet the most extreme consequences of Japan's economic weakness have not come to pass. Contrary to ominous predictions, the profound crisis in Tokyo's financial sector has not triggered an implosion of international capital markets. Japan's prolonged economic stagnation has not dragged the world into recession. Korea, Thailand, and other nations have rebounded from the Asian economic crisis without having to await Japan's recovery. And despite America's record trade deficit with Japan and the particular burden Japanese trade practices have imposed on individual U.S. industries, such as the steel industry, the U.S. economy has experienced unprecedented growth and record-low unemployment throughout Japan's economic stagnation.

Clearly, Japan's economic muddling does not necessarily forebode economic disaster and spreading trade wars. Nevertheless, a new U.S. president and American Congress will continue to give short shrift to the U.S.-Japan economic relationship—at some risk. It will be a high-stakes gamble to assume that the continued economic stagnation or even the prolonged anemic economic growth in the world's second-largest economy will continue having a benign influence on the global economy. Moreover, passive acceptance of Japan's performance denies Americans, Japanese, and the world unrealized opportunities and economic benefits of a healthier Japanese economy. This would be a heavy price for the world to pay.

GUIDING PRINICIPLES

In seeking to recast the U.S.-Japan economic relationship, the United States should be guided by the following principles:

Principle One: Pursue American Self-Interest

The United States has a profound self-interest in a strong, resilient Japanese economy that can be a market for U.S. products, a site for U.S. investment, a partner in fueling the global economic engine, a source of capital and technology, a reliable military ally, and an economically self-confident diplomatic peer. Americans should never be shy about articulating their interests or pursuing them with the Japanese. A new bilateral economic relationship can be built only on the self-assured pursuit of mutual advantage. Too many Americans believe that, in the past, U.S.-Japan relations were driven by U.S. altruism, not by the pursuit of U.S. self-interest. Such perceptions have undermined public support for the relationship. To be politically sustainable, any new American economic policy initiative with Japan must first have public trust. That support can best be built through selective, highly visible U.S. market-opening trade actions and other leveraging of Japanese restructuring.

Principle Two: Japanese Accountability

Japan has consistently failed to accept its moral and practical responsibility to pull its weight in an increasingly interdependent global economy. What were once purely domestic Japanese considerations—the functioning of Japan's retail distribution system, the application of Japanese antitrust law, the structure of the nation's postal savings system—now help determine the well-being of manufacturers in Korea hoping to sell to the Japanese market, of steelworkers in Wheeling, West Virginia, faced with competition from Japanese steelmakers, and of bond holders in New York and London. Japan no longer has the luxury of pursuing economic policies tailored solely to its own needs. And the pace and nature of Japanese economic restructuring must be measured by its impact on its trading partners, not simply against the backdrop of Japanese history and culture.

Principle Three: U.S.-Japanese Interdependence
The defining factor in the future of U.S.-Japan economic relations is the rapid and ongoing economic integration of the world's two largest economies. Two-way trade, investment, business alliances, and travel and cultural exchanges are on the rise. The United States and Japan are fated to share a common moment in history and a place on the global economic stage, so they have no choice but to work out their problems or find themselves perpetually in conflict and so much the poorer. The challenge facing policymakers in both Washington and Tokyo is to get ahead of the curve of economic integration and attempt to help shape it in order to maximize its potential and minimize its downsides.

Principle Four: Care and Humility
America's vulnerability to Japanese economic missteps must both animate America's effort in pursuit of Japanese reform and temper its assertiveness addressing Japan's economic choices. U.S. economic policy initiatives toward Japan must first do no harm.

Moreover, Japan's economic fate is ultimately in Japanese hands. Japan is most assuredly not the United States. American economic nostrums are not necessarily suited for Japanese society. The futile years spent pressuring Tokyo to lift its trade barriers and reform its domestic economy are a bitter lesson in the limits of U.S. influence over Japanese economic policy. The United States has repeatedly underestimated the inherent strength of the Japanese economy—in the immediate postwar period, in the wake of the 1970s oil shocks, and after the doubling of the value of the yen in 1985—and recent American predictions of Japan's economic demise have proved premature yet again. The United States should initiate a new era in U.S.-Japan economic relations—but it cannot mandate it.

U.S. LEADERSHIP

In recent debates over U.S. economic policy toward Japan, the dialogue has often been polarized between absolutes. For instance, either Japan's problems are a classic case of an under-performing economy, or these difficulties reflect deeper structural weaknesses that require a dismantling of Japan, Inc. Either the Japanese economy needs traditional fiscal pump priming, or the Bank of Japan (BOJ) should inflate its way out of recession. Either the United States should get tough with Japan in the face of a rising trade deficit, or it would only stir Japanese nationalism to kick them while they are down. Either the lesson from two decades of wrestling with Tokyo over trade problems is that progress can be made only on industry-specific issues, or the systemic nature of most individual trade tensions reinforces the need for structural negotiations. Either future U.S. trade conflicts with Japan must be resolved multilaterally, or the United States needs new unilateral tools to force changes in Japanese behavior.

As in most polarized debates, there are insights and useful policy prescriptions on both sides. In most instances in dealing with Japan, the choice for U.S. policy is not either/or but both. The challenge is to weave these disparate threads into a coherent pattern for U.S. economic policy toward Japan.

The common element among these opposing views is a firm belief that U.S. economic prosperity and its leadership in the world are integral to its relationship with Japan. The world's two largest economies have no choice but to work out a modus vivendi. In the 1980s, Japan prospered and America floundered. In the 1990s, these outcomes were reversed. But over the long haul, it is unlikely that the world's two largest economies can permanently remain on divergent economic paths. A second theme is that the United States should aggressively pursue its economic self-interest within that relationship. Passivity and inattention are unacceptable, whatever the distractions or the evidence that benign neglect may work in the short run as a default option.

The specific public policy initiatives that the United States can undertake to improve U.S.-Japan economic relations in the months and years ahead are laid out in detail in the following pages. Many of these proposals involve changes in Tokyo's policy that Washington should suggest, because they are in Japanese and American interests. Others involve unilateral changes in U.S. policy toward Japan as a means of strengthening the U.S. response to the ongoing Japanese economic challenge. And some involve joint efforts—including the creation of an open marketplace—to create a deeper, broader transpacific economic relationship in the future.

But despite the importance of all these proposals, the primary things the United States can do to prepare itself for the ups and downs of its single most important economic relationship rest solely in its hands. Even though these initiatives are not the focus of this study, they deserve mention as a reminder that the solution to most global problems starts at home. In that spirit, in recasting the U.S.-Japan economic relationship, the United States should remember to:

- *Run faster.* The United States will best contend with the economic challenges posed by Japan if it keeps its own economy strong, if its companies remain at the technological cutting edge, and if the American educational system and workforce continue to improve.

- *Save more.* The mushrooming U.S. trade deficit, of which the rising imbalance with Japan is the largest part, reflects the low level of domestic savings in the U.S. economy compared with U.S. demand for investment. Since recent American efforts to increase private savings have largely failed, decisions the next administration and the next Congress make about what to do with the federal budget surplus will largely determine the size of the future trade deficit.

In the end, Japan's problems must be solved by Japan. History suggests that Tokyo will eventually address the issues it confronts and that the Japanese economy will bounce back. It took

the United States more than a decade to deal with its "competitiveness problems" that first surfaced in the late 1970s. And during that period, many prognosticators were wrongly convinced that
America would never recover its former economic strength.

There is too much at stake in the pace and nature of Japan's current economic recovery to trust solely that time and good inten-
tions will create the Japan that the world and the United States
need. Rather, that goal requires a conscious refocusing of U.S. attention on Japan, backed by public policy initiatives to help Japan achieve
a healthier economy and ensure that American and global businesses share more fully in Japan's return to prosperity.

WHAT IS AT STAKE?

Japan and the United States are the world's two largest economies. In recent decades, the economic integration of these two commercial and financial behemoths has been slow but inexorable. Total U.S.-Japan trade has increased fourfold since 1980 and now accounts for 2.3 percent of U.S. GDP and 4.3 percent of Japanese GDP.[2] Japanese-owned firms in the United States employ 776,000 Americans, and U.S. firms in Japan employ 144,000 Japanese.[3]

The symbiotic economic relationship now evolving between the United States and Japan is graphically illustrated in capital markets. The Japanese supplied about a quarter of the funding for the U.S. current account deficit in 1998. And Japanese investors now own 7.2 percent of U.S. Treasury notes and a substantial portion of U.S. corporate stock.[4] Sustained U.S. economic growth in part requires continued Japanese willingness to provide funding to fuel that engine. Without it, U.S. interest rates could rise, the dollar could fall, and the strongest economic expansion in U.S. history could be impaired.

At the same time, Japan needs the United States, both as a safe and profitable haven in which to invest its excess capital, and paradoxically, as a source of entrepreneurial capital for its money-strapped companies. With low official interest rates, Japan needs the higher rates of return it can earn abroad if it is ever to find a way out of the crisis caused by its underfunded pension system and an insurance system with unfunded liabilities. Moreover, foreign capital—largely American—fueled the late 1990s rebound of the Tokyo Stock

---

[2]See, for example, www.ita.doc/gov/industry/otea/usftd/country.xls and the Council of Economic Advisors, *The Economic Report of the President 2000* (Washington, D.C.: U.S. Government Printing Office, February 2000).

[3]See www.ita.doc.gov/industry/otea/usftd/country.xls and The World Bank, *World Development Report* (Washington, D.C., August 1999).

[4]See www.ustreas.gov/tic/sl_42609.txt.

Exchange (TSE). This run-up in asset values probably did nearly as much as the government's bank bailout to give Tokyo's beleaguered financial institutions some much-needed breathing room. And American investors are leading the wave of mergers and acquisitions that is reshaping the Japanese corporate landscape.

This economic interdependence is vulnerable to how Japan unwinds its current economic crisis. If Japan simply muddles through with sluggish domestic demand for imports and continued dependence on exports, the U.S. trade deficit with Japan will continue to rise, and the U.S. foreign debt—which needs to be funded by borrowing abroad—will mount. If Tokyo gets its recovery terribly wrong and recession slides into depression, a fire sale of U.S. assets by panicky Japanese financial institutions could help burst the Wall Street bubble. For Japan, if the economy continues to stagnate, American ardor for Japanese stocks and corporate investment will eventually wane. In fact, it was the pullout of American money in the spring 2000 that sent the Japanese stock market tumbling again.

TRADE AND INVESTMENT

U.S. exporters and investors have a particular stake in Japan's economic recovery and in the nature of that turnaround.

In 1999, the United States ran a $74 billion trade deficit with Japan—becoming America's largest bilateral deficit, roughly a third of the total U.S. goods and services trade imbalance with the world.[5] From a macroeconomic standpoint, bilateral trade imbalances are not terribly significant. But in the past, they have proven to be a political lightening rod, a symbol to the American public and to U.S. political leaders of a "troubled" relationship. Moreover, the persistence of the U.S. deficit with Japan and the continued poor performance of U.S. exporters to Japan suggest that deficit is an indicator of a deeper problem in the relationship, one that has to do with Japan's parsimonious nature as an importer.

---

[5]See www.ita.doc.gov/industry/otea/usftd/country.xls.

Compared with a quarter century ago, the Japanese marketplace is now much more open to imports and foreign direct investment (FDI). But relative to the performance of other major industrial economies, Japan remains the most closed market in the world. Imports account for a mere 18 percent of domestic consumption of manufactured products in Japan, compared with 37 percent in the United States and 30 percent in Germany.[6] The relatively closed nature of Japan's market is strikingly apparent in the steel industry. Japanese steel imports account for just 7 percent of apparent consumption, compared with 49 percent in Germany, 48 percent in the United Kingdom, and 25 percent in the United States.[7]

As a result, while manufactured goods make up 90 percent of U.S. exports to Germany and 92 percent of exports to France, they account for only 72 percent of U.S. exports to Japan.[8] Such differences are significant because Japan's market, even in the depths of a recession, is about as big as that of Germany, France, and Britain combined. So for the U.S. economy—which now derives one-third of its recent growth and one-quarter of its recent job creation from exports—even marginal differences in market openness to America's value-added products hurt U.S. producers and workers.

Japanese officials are quick to argue that these differences in import penetration merely reflect the preferences of Japanese consumers. But Japanese prices for a wide range of goods and services are consistently higher than those in the United States. In 1998, for example, a Japanese refrigerator was 2.9 times more expensive per cubic unit of capacity than an American one. Cardiac pace makers were 6.9 times as expensive. And there were similar price disparities for basic materials such as steel and cement.[9] Given such persistent price differentials, if the Japanese market was free of import barriers, entrepreneurs could turn a quick profit by buying goods

---

[6]Edward J. Lincoln, *Troubled Times* (Washington, DC: Brookings Institution, 1999), p. 23.

[7]Mark Tilton, "Japan's Steel Cartel and the 1998 Steel Export Surge," A Japan Information Access Project Working Paper, October 23, 1998.

[8]See www.ita.doc.gov.

[9]Edward J. Lincoln, "Whither Trade Policy with Japan?: A Position Paper for the CFR Study Group," October 1999, p. 5.

in the United States and reselling them to Japan. The fact that this gray market does not exist strongly suggests that the Japanese market is still walled-off by a host of nontariff trade barriers.

Similarly, the Japanese economy is relatively closed to FDI. The 1998 cumulative total of FDI in Japan is equal to only 1.1 percent of Japan's GDP. By comparison, FDI is equal to 7.3 percent of GDP in Germany and 8.5 percent in the United States.

Foreign investment in Japan has picked up dramatically in recent years. It soared from $3.8 billion in 1998 to $12.7 billion in 1999.[10] Renault now has a controlling interest in Nissan. Similar changes have been seen in the financial sector. Merrill Lynch has acquired Yamaichi Securities. These headline-grabbing investments are historic breakthroughs. But statistically, they must be seen in perspective. Although FDI in Japan tripled in 1999, it was still little more than that flowing into Mexico, a country whose economy is one-tenth Japan's size. At last count, the United States still had only $19 billion invested in Japan, compared with the $124 billion Japan invested in the United States. To put the recent flurry of inward investment activity in some perspective, total FDI in Japan from all sources would have to grow by more than $500 billion just to reach a "global standard" comparable to that of other industrial nations. To reach that level any time soon would require the foreign purchase of the equivalent of Toyota, Honda, Sony, Canon, and a host of other major Japanese firms.[11]

Foreign mergers and acquisitions are also on the rise, with 61 instances of foreign firms buying Japanese companies in the first half of 1999 alone, representing 13.8 percent of all mergers and acquisitions in Japan—up from 7.6 percent in 1993. But the number of foreign companies acquired by Japanese firms still exceeded foreign mergers and acquisitions by 50 percent, suggesting that the real beneficiaries of Japan's recession-driven restructuring are still the larger Japanese corporations.

---

[10]Douglas Ostrom, "Japan's Current Account Surplus Contracted in 1999 But Numbers Still Worrisome," Japan Economic Institute (JEI) Report, No. 8B, February 25, 2000, p. 6.

[11]Jesper Koll, "Strategic Investments in Japan: The Economics of Opportunity and the Politics of Obstacles" (Tokyo: Jesper Koll Research, January 12, 1999).

The American economy and individual U.S. companies pay a heavy price for this continued shortfall in U.S. investment in Japan. The overseas arms of U.S. companies spur exports. Without a local capability for distribution and after-sales service, no American firm can build a large market share in Japan. Although 26 percent of total U.S. exports go to foreign affiliates of U.S. firms, only 16 percent of U.S. exports to Japan are generated by trade between affiliates of the same firm. Sales by their Japanese affiliates could compensate U.S. companies for their shortfall in exports—but they do not. Only about 3 percent of domestic corporate sales in Japan are made by the affiliates of foreign-owned firms. By comparison, such companies account for more than 9 percent of total corporate sales in the United States.[12]

American companies are also disadvantaged by the "sanctuary nature" of the domestic Japanese market. The growth and competitive success of cutting-edge American industries are inextricably linked to their ability to sell abroad. Any restraint on their chances of selling into a $4 trillion market is a concern—not so much because of the immediate impact on jobs in the United States but because of the dynamic impact on profitability, economies of scale, the productivity-enhancing benefits of greater competition, and the benefits of staying in touch with the technological and product advances of their competitors. This is currently less of a competitive need than it was a decade ago, given the current lead American high-technology firms enjoy over Japanese firms. But there is no telling how long that lead will last.

More broadly, there is a systemic cost to the demonstration effect of the Japanese economy. Japanese practices—industrial policy and other forms of government intervention in the market—have long been a model for the rest of Asia. Japan's postwar, government-directed economic development was the paradigm for Korea and Taiwan. China has self-consciously mimicked Japan's support for "strategic" industries, such as consumer electronics and automobiles. If Japan succeeds in muddling through its current economic difficulties and reviving its economy without significant

---

[12]Lincoln, *Troubled Times*, p. 88.

restructuring or deregulation, the message to the rest of Asia will be that business as usual is back, that the "development state" is still a valid paradigm, and that tough economic decisions can be avoided.

Similarly, the multilateral trading system is built on the assumption that market mechanisms determine competitive outcomes. Over time, if Japan is allowed to behave otherwise, continuing to "free ride" on the liberal trading order, it will undermine its commitment to the multilateral system, both in the United States and around the world.

THE ASIAN CORNERSTONE

The United States also has a major stake in Japan's economic recovery because of the critical role Japan's economy plays in Asia. Japan is by far the largest economy in Asia, accounting for 70 percent of the East Asian marketplace. Its economy is 7 times the size of China's, and 10 times the size of South Korea's.

The revivals of the Thai and Korean economies in 1999, while the Japanese economy remained in serious crisis, caught many economists by surprise. Most analysts assumed that East Asia could not recover in the absence of a Japanese rebound. Clearly, internal restructuring, the resumption of domestic demand, and exports to other regions—notably the United States—permitted Asian recovery in spite of Japan's stagnation. How sustainable those recoveries are in the absence of a Japanese revival has yet to be seen.

For example, in 1999 Japanese imports from Asia rose 2.7 percent. But they still remained 8 percent below their 1997 peak. Curtailed Japanese demand shifted the burden of the export-led recoveries of Korea, Thailand, and Indonesia onto the United States, whose imports from Asia grew by 11 percent in 1999. As a result, while the United States ran a cumulative trade deficit with Asia of $465 billion from 1997 to 1999, Japan ran a cumulative trade surplus of $189 billion with the rest of Asia over the same period.[13]

---

[13]See www.ita.doc.gov/td/industry/otea/usfth/aggregate/H99to8.txt and www.jetro.go.jp/it/e/pub/whitepaper/trade.pdf.

Furthermore, after bankrolling much of Asia's economic miracle, Japanese FDI in Asia and Japanese bank financing for Asia have dried up, thanks to Japan's economic woes. From 1995 to 1997, Japanese firms ploughed an average of 1.33 trillion yen ($11 billion) a year into Asia. But in 1998, they invested only 840 billion yen ($7 billion).[14] Moreover, in June 1997, immediately prior to Thailand's collapse, Japanese banks owed $123.8 billion in outstanding loans to Asia. By June 1999, that lending had fallen by 40 percent.[15]

Not only whether but how Japan recovers may prove critical to Asia's long-term prospects. Under current conditions, for example, with low import penetration and low elasticity of demand for imports, even if Japan were to grow an unrealistic 5 percent per year, South Korea's annual growth would lift by only 0.2 percent and Thailand's by 0.3 percent.

Moreover, the nature of Japan's ongoing corporate restructuring will impact recovery efforts in the rest of Asia. For example, of Mitsubishi Electric Corporation's announced job cuts, two out of five, or 6,100, will occur outside Japan. Thai and Filipino workers, not Japanese workers, will pay a large share of the price for overcapacity and overindebtedness in Japan. As newspaper accounts from Tokyo never fail to note, joblessness is a psychological trauma for Japanese workers accustomed to lifelong employment. It is no less a trauma for workers in other countries.

Finally, the United States needs Japan to continue bankrolling Asian development, something Washington has long abandoned. In 1998, Tokyo gave $5.3 billion in foreign aid to Asian nations, making it the largest regional donor of foreign assistance. In addition, through the Miyazawa Plan, Japan made $30 billion available in short- and long-term loans for the region. Without such aid, the disparity between the haves and the have-nots in much of Asia will only grow. Without an eventual economic recovery and the government revenues it produces, Japan's ability to continue providing such massive aid will be difficult to sustain.

---

[14]"Statistical Profile: International Transaction of Japan in 1998," *JEI Report*, No. 35, September 17, 1999.

[15]Douglas Ostrom, "Tokyo's Changing Role in Financial Markets: Taking a Step Backward?" *JEI Report*, No. 43, November 12, 1999.

A SECURITY LYNCHPIN

In an uncertain region—with North Korea always capable of destabilizing northeast Asia, China periodically menacing Taiwan, and ongoing instability in Indonesia—a militarily strong Japan is the lynchpin of Asian security.

Since World War II, Japan has never spent much more than one percent of its GDP on defense. Because of domestic fears of a return to militarism and the sensitivities of Japan's neighbors, Tokyo is unlikely to spend a greater portion of its economy on security anytime soon. In fact, sluggish growth has already led some Japanese opinion leaders to call for a cutback in host-nation support, the money Tokyo contributes to the maintenance of U.S. forces in Japan. The only foreseeable way for Japan to mean-ingfully increase its contribution to future regional security is through economic growth. Only in an expanding economy will defense spending be able to increase in nominal terms without break-ing through the current one percent ceiling.

The United States would be an indirect beneficiary of a well-funded Japanese regional security role. A growing portion of U.S. trade and investment is with East Asia. Political tensions or out-right conflict in the region would threaten those economic ties, with severe consequences for the domestic U.S. economy. The bur-den of being the sole provider of commercial stability in the region has already begun to wear on Washington. To shoulder more of that burden, the Japanese economy must grow.

A MULTI-PRONGED STRATEGY

U.S. economic policy toward Japan must necessarily be two-pronged: short-term and long-term, macroeconomic and microeconomic, systemic and sector-specific, practical and visionary, and supportive and challenging—in other words, it should offer both carrots and sticks. It can neither ignore the changes going on in Japan nor accept them at face value. Out of initial necessity, the new U.S. president must continue to prod and advise the Japanese government on immediate efforts to revive the Japanese economy through fiscal pump priming, expediting deregulation and industrial restructuring, and addressing pressing market-access concerns. But if that is the limit of the new administration's Japan vision, it will ultimately fail. To accommodate the accelerating integration of the U.S. and Japanese economies, to anticipate the problems that are likely to emerge with the advent of a new Japanese economy, and to break with the fractious past and chart a smoother course for U.S.-Japan relations in the future, the next U.S. government should launch a bold initiative to create an open marketplace between Japan and the United States by a date certain.

STIMULATE THE ECONOMY

For Japan, the 1990s was a lost decade. Growth averaged one percent, compared with a world average of 3.4 percent. In 2000, the output gap for Japan's economy—the difference between how fast the economy was actually growing and how fast it was capable of growing—was expected to be 4.6 percent, the worst performance by any major industrial nation in the last decade.[16]

The cost of flat growth and recession was devastating. Asset prices collapsed. A homeowner in one of Japan's six largest cities saw the

---

[16] *World Economic Outlook*, International Monetary Fund, April 2000.

value of his residence fall 60 percent since its peak in 1990. The owner of an office building in one of those metropolitan regions saw her investment shrink by 80 percent. The stock market fell to one-third of its previous value during the bubble economy of the late 1980s, wiping out paper fortunes that had been the foundation for unsupportable lifestyles. Housing starts fell to a decade low, as did new passenger car sales. Unemployment more than doubled to reach a postwar record, with new prospects that joblessness could double again. And for the first time in more than a generation, Japan suffered some of the same social travail—rising divorces, domestic violence, suicides—that have long plagued other economically troubled societies.

The first sign of a way out came with strong economic growth in the first half of 1999. The Tokyo stock market experienced a modest recovery, thanks in part to foreign investors' newfound faith in Japanese equities. Japanese banks could borrow again overseas without paying a debilitating premium. And there was some pickup in consumer spending. But these hopes were shattered when the economy shrank again in the second half of the year, casting Japan back into recession.

The economy again rebounded in the first half of 2000, but it was unclear whether the recovery had legs. Business investment and consumer spending remained weak. The Tokyo stock market soared over 20,000, up from just 13,000 in the fall of 1998, its revival was on the wings of a handful of high-technology and Internet stocks and did not reflect an overall return of investor confidence in Japanese corporations as demonstrated by the fact that the market tumbled in spring 2000.

Japan's overriding challenge is to halt this yo-yoing of the economy and achieve sustainable growth. Consumer and investor confidence is a direct function of economic prospects. The political and social obstacles to further economic restructuring will all be easier to overcome if new jobs are being created and incomes are expanding. Fiscal stimulus is a fool's errand if it is merely a substitute for structural reform. But in the short run, it remains indispensable to avoid a recurrence of recession.

A New Beginning

Experience over the last decade demonstrates that if enough money is pumped into the economy, expansion will follow. In fiscal year 1998, Tokyo increased spending by 10.3 trillion yen ($85.8 billion). As a direct result, nearly half the growth from the first quarter of 1999 came from public works spending. When that spending petered out in the latter half of 1999, growth contracted. Tokyo had a similar experience when increased public spending in 1995 led to strong growth in 1996.

Tokyo has a checkered history of economic pump priming. Flush with success from 1995, Tokyo returned to a contractionary budget in 1996, which helped choke the recovery. Throughout most of the 1990s, Japan has generally spent much less as a portion of its GDP on economic stimulus than any other major industrial nation facing recession. And except for in 1995 and 1998, Tokyo has made a habit of spending far less on stimulus that it announced it would spend, raising expectations that are never fulfilled.[17] For example, the budget adopted by the Diet in March 2000 was 4.3 percent smaller than total budgetary spending in 1999, including both the initial and supplemental outlays.

One explanation for this erratic behavior is the fear of sustained deficit spending, especially by the Ministry of Finance (MOF). Japan is now the world's largest debtor nation, its total government debt having surpassed that of the United States in 1999. The annual public sector deficit is more than 10 percent of GDP. The ratio of gross government debt to GDP will be 129 percent of GDP in fiscal year 2000, the highest level among all major industrial countries.[18] And debt forecasts for Japan are even grimmer than they were for the United States in the early 1990s.

Optimists argue that as the second-richest country in the world, Japan has little trouble borrowing this money and can afford to service such deficit spending. If public spending and eco-

---

[17]Adam S. Posen, *Restoring Japan's Economic Growth* (Washington, D.C.: Institute for International Economics, 1998), p. 42.

[18]*Oriental Economist*, "Fiscal Debilitation," March 2000, Volume 68, No. 3, p. 3, and *JEI Report*, March 31, 2000.

nomic restructuring work, the economy will pick up, the need to borrow will go down, and the debt and the deficit will once again be more manageable. Pessimists point out that once debt reaches critical mass, the effect of compound interest rates makes it exceedingly difficult for nations to climb out of the holes they have dug for themselves.

Japan's debt burden has already been a source of problems. In 1999, Moody's, the bond-rating agency, downgraded Japanese government debt from the risk-free rating of AAA to Aa1. Although largely a symbolic gesture, Moody's indicated that it was considering a further downgrading. Moreover, in late 1998 when the government's Trust Fund Bureau announced that it would temporarily suspend buying government bonds, the financial market panicked in the face of the deficit and drove up long-term interest rates. A repeat move could throttle recovery.

Japan's deficit absorbs domestic savings that might otherwise be available to foreigners. If at some point markets decide that Japanese bond yields and the value of the yen should reflect the seriousness of Japan's fiscal situation, the United States will pay a price. A higher Japanese interest rate would make financing the U.S. current account deficit more costly, and a weaker yen would play havoc with the U.S. trade balance.

With such constraints on spending, Tokyo's other fiscal lever has been tax policy. But in recent years, Japan has pursued a contradictory approach to taxes. Many analysts blame the 1997 rise in the consumption tax, from 3 to 5 percent, for throwing cold water on the 1996 recovery. Since then, the government has raised taxes by 15.8 trillion yen ($132 billion) and cut them by a total of 17.3 trillion ($144 billion), hardly an expansionary tax policy.[19]

U.S. moral suasion regarding Japanese fiscal policy is necessarily limited. It is the Japanese taxpayer, not an American one, who must ultimately foot the bill for government spending. With that cau-

---

[19]Adam S. Posen, *Restoring Japan's Economic Growth*.

tionary note in mind, Washington should urge Tokyo to do the following:

- *Maintain public spending to keep the economy on a sustainable growth path.* To avoid stop-start growth, in the short run the government budget should not have a contractionary effect on the economy. Growth will enable the economy to finance debt. To maximize the benefit of such spending for Japanese consumers, Tokyo should refocus spending away from rural construction projects toward meeting urban and information infrastructure needs.

- *Be mindful of the increase in the public debt.* Tokyo should not use fiscal pump priming as an alternative to biting the bullet on economic deregulation, which will have a more sustainable long-term economic stimulus effect.

- *Cut taxes.* Japan's own Economic Strategy Council, appointed to advise the prime minister, recommended that "taxation needs to be reformed to become neutral to economic activities." Lower personal income taxes would spur consumption with the least possible distortionary effect. Corporate tax cuts are less of a priority, because although the corporate income tax rate is higher than that in the United States, two-thirds of all companies do not pay any taxes. Consumption taxes, at least for consumer durables, might also be reduced, with a phased reimposition announced ahead of time to encourage consumers to front-load purchases. The proposal for mortgage deductibility initially included in then Prime Minister Keizo Obuchi's November 1998 stimulus package should be revived.

REVIVE THE FINANCIAL SECTOR

The banking and financial infrastructure of any country is the circulatory system of its economy. In Japan, these arteries have been clogged for some time, thus constraining growth. Recent angioplasty has relieved much of the patient's distress. But the financial system is far from recovery.

The origins of Japan's current banking problems lie in the asset-price inflation of the late 1980s, when banks increased lending to real estate projects and small and medium-sized companies that collateralized their loans with real estate. Such practices fueled the real estate and stock market bubble that eventually crashed in 1990 when interest rates rose. In the wake of the collapse, banks were left holding the bag. At the end of September 1999, the seventeen largest Japanese banks had 19.1 trillion yen ($159 billion) in bad loans on their books.[20] Banks burdened by such debt first chose to save themselves by curtailing credit. Domestic lending by commercial banks began declining at the end of 1995, and by late 1996, banks were taking in more money than they were releasing. By 1999, lending was contracting by about 5 percent per year. Thanks to their efforts to clean up their books, bank lending was about 4 percent less than might have been expected under existing economic conditions, interest rates, and other factors.[21] This cutoff of credit had a devastating effect on the economy, especially for small and medium-sized firms that needed capital to stay in business.

The fragility of the financial system also had a devastating impact on consumer spending. Fearful that money deposited in a bank might not be retrievable if the institution went belly-up, many Japanese began keeping their savings in home safes—denying it to the commercial credit system through which it could be re-lent, spurring growth. Wary of the fate of their pensions, mindful of falling prices, fearful they might lose their jobs, consumers did the only prudent thing: they saved more. (Japan's 23 percent personal savings rate far exceeded that of any other industrial nation. In Germany, for example, the rate was only 15 percent.)

Finally, the Japanese government and business community began to deal with its banking problem. The Long-Term Credit Bank of Japan and Nippon Credit Bank were nationalized. Thanks to $62.5 billion of public funds injected into the banking system, fifteen of the sixteen major banks reporting data for fiscal years

[20]Jon Choy, "Japan Banks Report Mixed Results as Industry Restructuring Proceeds," *JEI Report*, No. 46B, December 10, 1999, p. 4.
[21]"Japan Selected Issues," *IMF Staff Country Report*, No. 98/113, International Monetary Fund, October 1998.

1997 and 1998 improved their capital-to-asset ratios.[22] Banks cut their volume of nonperforming loans by nearly 10 percent between March 1999 and September 1999.[23] Initially scorned as beholden to the Ministry of Finance, the Financial Supervisory Agency—set up to restructure the banking system—proved remarkably independent and effective. The August 1999 merger of the Industrial Bank of Japan (IBJ), Dai-Ichi Kangyo Bank, and Fuji Bank will eventually create the world's largest financial holding company and could signal the beginning of a long-overdue shakeout in the banking sector. The revival of the stock market helped spur a dramatic improvement in the value of bank shares, turning billions of dollars in negative assets into positive ones.

But the financial system as a whole was far from healthy. Much of the banks' debt problems had merely been shifted from their own balance sheets to the government's, which by mid-1999 found itself the guarantor of 12 percent of all bank loans to corporations. Even with an accelerated effort to write off bad loans, it would take six years to sell all the banks' bad debts.[24] As the banks slowly worked their way out from underneath their mountains of debt, the long-term threats to economic stability increasingly became Japan's tottering insurance companies and pension funds. Nissan Life collapsed in 1997, and Toho Mutual Life went bankrupt in June 1999. Other insurance companies had substantial unrealized losses on foreign real estate investments that had gone sour. Moreover, they had significant holdings of foreign securities that were unhedged against foreign exchange risks.

In addition, Japanese corporations had up to 100 trillion yen ($955.6 billion) in unfunded pension liabilities. This shortfall is attributable to years of poor returns. Companies have long limited their contributions to their pension reserves based on the assumption that existing reserves were earning a 5.5 percent annual return. In fact, Japan's long-term government bonds—a favored invest-

---

[22]Jon Choy, "Japanese Banks Drop Bad Loans," *JEI Report*, No. 18B, May 7, 1999, p. 6.

[23]Jon Choy, "Japan Banks Report Mixed Results as Industry Restructuring Proceeds," *JEI Report*, No. 46B, December 10, 1999, p. 4.

[24]*Oriental Economist*, September 1999.

ment for pension fund managers—have not yielded that assumed rate of return for years. So every year the gap between available pension funds and future needs has widened. This problem will become fully evident when Japanese companies must report pension fund assets and liabilities beginning in April 2001.[25]

How Japan manages or mismanages its financial sector is of critical concern to the United States. The ongoing fragility of the banking system and the profound weakness of insurance companies and pension funds make the Japanese financial system particularly vulnerable to panics. A sudden downturn in the stock market and bank shares—triggered by unrest in China or trouble with North Korea, a further contraction of the economy or a major bankruptcy—could lead to repatriation of capital to shore up positions at home. (Eventually, such Japanese funds would probably filter back to the United States, where they could generate better returns. Nevertheless, a sudden movement of Japanese funds in the short run could cause a decline in American stock and bond markets and higher U.S. interest rates.)

Of course, as with fiscal policy, cleaning up Japan's financial sector is a Japanese responsibility. But since the rest of the world could pay dearly if Tokyo gets it wrong, Washington should take the following initiatives:

- *Encourage Tokyo to speed up the write-off of bad bank loans.* The value of bank loans that were deemed unrecoverable or unlikely to be repaid fell by 17.5 percent from the end of March 1999 to the end of September 1999.[26] This trend should not slacken; getting bad loans off corporation books will encourage mergers and acquisitions and foreign investment

- *Press Tokyo for faster financial deregulation.* This would foster more competition for Japan's huge savings pool (including the money in the postal savings system that began to become available in

---

[25]"Ministry of Finance Orders Corporate Japan to Disclose Pension Liabilities," *Japan Daily Digest*, Volume XI, Issue 48, March 17, 2000.
[26]Jon Choy, "Japanese Banks Past Worst of Nonperforming Loan Problems," *JEI Report*, No. 6B, February 11, 2000.

2000) and a more efficient use of these savings. Nomura Research Institute estimates that if Japanese pension funds could achieve only an 8.5 percent rate of return, they could be self-sustaining. That return may be possible only if many of those funds are moved abroad. In fiscal year 1998, corporate pension funds moved 525 billion yen into foreign-managed trust accounts—a 45 percent increase over fiscal year 1997. But this sum represents less than one-half of one percent of all financial assets in the country.[27]

- *Urge Japan to improve financial supervision.* Tokyo cannot run a twenty-first century financial market with nineteenth-century levels of expertise. Japan has one-eighth the number of accountants that work in Britain but has an economy two-and-a-half times larger. The U.S. Federal Deposit Insurance Corporation (FDIC) has 1,800 examiners; Japan has 658. Such disparities in oversight contributed to Japan's recent banking problems. As Tokyo creates new financial mechanisms—such as the Japanese Nasdaq, which opened June 19, 2000—the potential for new forms of corruption will multiply. A failure to exert proper supervision over these activities could undermine public trust in the very institutions being created to help rectify financial sector problems from the past.

- *Tighten U.S. supervision of Japanese financial institutions.* In September 1998 the U.S. Federal Reserve, in conjunction with the BOJ, asked Japanese banks operating in the United States to report on their financial situation every four weeks—disclosing holdings in U.S. treasuries, outstanding loans and commitments, and dollar credit lines with U.S. banks. This oversight should continue and be broadened where appropriate.

- *The Federal Reserve should act as the buyer of first resort.* If Japanese financial institutions find themselves in trouble again and move to sell off large holdings of U.S. bonds, the Federal Reserve should act to shore up the market.

---

[27]"Pension Funds Moved Yen 525 Billion Into Foreign Trust Banks in FY '98," *Japan Daily Digest*, Volume X, No. 87, May 18, 1999.

PURSUE A CAUTIOUS MONETARY AND EXCHANGE RATE POLICY

With interest rates hovering barely above zero for years, adjusting the official cost of money—the BOJ's traditional tool for exercising monetary policy and stimulating the economy—has been ineffective. Moreover, the BOJ's open market operations have not led to greater bank lending because there has been no demand for such credit.

Faced with this policy impasse and with deflationary pressures, American economists, such as Paul Krugman and Adam Posen, have long argued that Japan is in a liquidity trap and that the only way out is to raise inflationary expectations through a sharp increase in the money supply. They contend that the BOJ should set an explicit inflation target for the Japanese economy and print sufficient money so that prices rise by that amount. They contend that consumers and corporations, seeing higher inflation coming, will boost expenditures, rekindling economic growth. Japan's Ministry of Finance and the holders of Japanese bonds have argued that such a strategy either will not work or will create instability in currency markets and spark uncontrollable inflation that will wipe out the value of their holdings.

The cost of money in Japan will have an impact on the yen-dollar exchange rate. The value of the yen has long been a major shaping force in U.S.-Japan economic relations. Tokyo views a strong yen as a threat to economic recovery. Japan's Economic Planning Agency estimates that a 10 percent increase in the yen's value could knock 0.5 percent off of Japan's annual economic growth. At the same time, the failure of Japanese industry to restructure despite the depth of the recent recession is in part traceable to the prolonged weakness of the yen. When the yen was valued at 80 to the dollar for a brief period in the mid-1990s, the high cost of doing business by relying solely on domestically made components, rather than on the relatively less-expensive imported parts, began to fracture *keiretsu* relationships in the Japanese auto and electronics industries, accelerating the movement of production capacity abroad. After the United States intervened in currency markets in 1995 to weaken the yen and help spur Japan's domestic economy, the restructuring pressure was relieved. In 1999, the yen appreciated again by 14.9 percent. The BOJ's sporadic efforts to weaken, or at least stabilize, the yen in part reflected Tokyo's desire to spur economic recovery through export-led growth, with obvious consequences for the U.S.-Japan trade balance. Thus a weak yen facilitates economic muddling through, permitting Japan to achieve some modicum of growth without a major structural reform of its economy.

In the long run, the International Monetary Fund (IMF) expects a 20 to 30 percent appreciation of the yen due to an expected decline in Japanese savings as the population ages. With lower savings, the Japanese current account surplus will shrink. With less of a surplus that must be invested abroad, the yen will strengthen.

But in the medium-term, the IMF expects continued downward pressure on the yen, given an anticipated interest rate differential between Japan and the United States that will shift capital out of yen-denominated holdings and into dollar-denominated assets, especially as high-yielding postal savings accounts become due in the years ahead.

There is no question that unchecked yen strength could threaten Japan's recovery. A rapid increase in the yen's value could retard the restoration of corporate profitability—which is largely based on exports—thus undermining business investments and consumer spending that would short-circuit economic growth. But that threat should not be exaggerated. It merely argues for a slow-paced appreciation.

Underlying economic fundamentals and the needs of the rest of the world necessitate a stronger yen. Japan's recovery must be sustainable. And sustainability is possible only through permanent restructuring of the Japanese economy. A stronger yen will force Tokyo policymakers to accelerate economic reform and will encourage Japanese corporate managers to focus on profits, not on market share. A stronger yen will send the right price signals to businesses, encouraging a shift in investment away from export-dependent industrial sectors toward the long-neglected domestic service sector, which is less vulnerable to the exchange rate. A stronger yen will guard against a premature tightening of both monetary and fiscal policy by the Japanese government. And a strong yen will help boost economic recovery in the rest of Asia by increasing Japanese imports of regional goods and by spurring Japanese investment in the region. (Nomura Research Institute estimates that a 1 percent strengthening of the yen against the dollar boosts Korea's GDP by 0.26 percent and Taiwan's economy by 0.17 percent.)[28]

The yen-dollar exchange rate has long been a point of contention in U.S.-Japan economic relations. The record buildup of the U.S. trade deficit in the mid-1980s eventually led to the Plaza Accord and a doubling of the yen's value. Subsequently, U.S. manufacturers have periodically pressed Washington to manage the exchange rate to limit what they allege is "unfair" competition from a weak yen. But in recent years, the strength of the U.S. economy and the benefits of a strong dollar have quieted concerns in Detroit or Pittsburgh about the rising U.S. trade deficit with Japan and the role the relatively weak yen may have played in that imbalance. And there is little to no support in the business community, on Capitol Hill, or in the U.S. Treasury for U.S. intervention in currency markets to strengthen the yen.

Therefore, for sound economic and political reasons, markets should be left to determine the yen's value. But given the complications any weakening of the yen would pose for U.S.-Japan trade relations, the secretary of the Treasury should:

- Consult widely and regularly with industry members and members of Congress on the impact of the exchange rate on the U.S. economy.

- Monitor the impact on the yen of increasing the Japanese money supply. A weaker yen could drive up the U.S. trade deficit with Japan and have deleterious knock-on effects on the currencies of Asia, especially the pivotal Hong Kong dollar. It was the weakening of the yen (and the strengthening of the dollar) in 1995

---

[28]*Oriental Economist*, "Strong Yen Helps Asia," September 1999, p.3.

that some analysts believe set the stage for the 1997 Asian financial crisis. A significant yen devaluation would be an unacceptable consequence of reflating the Japanese economy.

- Make clear to Tokyo that a strong economy and a weak yen are incompatible with Japan's responsibilities to the world. The strength of the yen should reflect Japan's economic fundamentals.

ACCELERATE ECONOMIC RESTRUCTURING

There is no doubt that the economic trauma of the last decade is changing the Japanese business landscape. But restructuring has been slow and has avoided tackling major structural problems. It is hardly comparable to the trauma and transformations experienced by other major industrial nations trying to dig their way out of prolonged recessions. As a result, much of the uphill struggle to mold a new Japanese economy still lies ahead.

Signs of a new Japan appear daily. A venture capital market has developed where one never existed before. Softbank, the darling of the Western press, has set up a 150 billion yen venture capital fund. Nikko Securities has a 50-70 billion yen fund to buy stakes in Japanese startup companies. And Fuji Bank has put 20 billion yen into management buyouts as corporate Japan restructures.[29] A Japanese Nasdaq will finally help channel the savings of noodle shop owners into high-flying Internet companies.

But the hype surrounding such developments has gotten ahead of the reality. Japan has fewer than 100 venture capital firms with about $6.7 billion in assets, compared with more than 500 such firms in the United States with nearly $100 billion in assets.[30] More important, most Japanese venture capital firms are affiliates of banks and insurance companies (while most U.S. venture capital com-

[29]*Economist Intelligence Unit*, Country Reports, February 25, 2000.
[30]David Hale, "The Global Economic Observer," Zurich Financial Services, Chicago, Ill., January 2000.

panies are independent), and they have their parents' conservative investment strategies: committing only 10 percent of their funds to the technology sector, compared with 78 percent in the United States. As a result, although Japanese investment in high technology grew an impressive 12.7 percent in 1999, all such developments are relative. In the same period, U.S. high-tech investment grew 21.9 percent on a base that was twice as large.[31]

Similarly, old-line corporate Japan is much more aggressive today about cutting costs than at any time in the past. The market-driven process of creative destruction has finally begun. In the first half of 1999, there were 440 corporate mergers and acquisitions in Japan, up 20 percent from the year before and nearly double the value of all mergers and acquisitions activity for 1998.[32] This trend has major implications for important sectors, such as telecommunications. For example, DDI Corp., KDD Corp., and IDO Corp. have announced plans to merge, creating Japan's second-largest telecommunications group. Principal banks—such as Fuji, Daiwa, Sakura, and Sumitomo—have announced that, in a break with recent practice, they will liquidate some of their shareholdings in major borrowers. Nippon Credit Bank Mitsui Marine & Fire Insurance, Japan's third-largest casualty insurer, will merge with the fifth-largest, Nippon Fire & Marine, and the eighth-largest, Koa Fire & Marine—creating the country's biggest insurer.

The labor force is becoming more flexible, with nearly a quarter of the workforce now employed part-time, up from 16 percent in 1987.[33] In the most recent nationwide private sector wage negotiations—or *shunto*—unions agreed to record-low pay hikes.

Renault's announced restructuring of Nissan could well prove a watershed development. Three plants will be closed, cutting grossly underutilized production capacity by 31 percent. The number of suppliers will be cut in half. And 16,500 jobs will be eliminated. Parts will henceforth be sourced from all over the world. Nis-

[31]"IT Investment Grew 12.7% in '99, But Only 60% as Fast as U.S.," *Japan Daily Digest*, March 13, 2000.

[32]"FRC: New Weakness Could Trigger Takeover of Recapitalized Banks," *Japan Daily Digest*, Volume X, Issue 116, June 28, 1999.

[33]"Japan Selected Issues," International Monetary Fund, October 1998.

san will also sell most of the shares it holds in nearly 1,400 other companies. Capacity utilization is expected to rise from 53 percent to 77 percent, making Nissan competitive with other international car companies.[34]

But as Nissan President Yoshikazu Hanawa said when announcing his firm's restructuring, "Ninety-five percent of the work remains."[35] And in June 1999, the *Financial Times* opined, "[Restructuring] trends should not be exaggerated. They remain tentative, and very much limited to the largest and most internationally exposed companies. Many restructurings have been more notable for rhetoric than action. In those industries that do not face immediate financial pressure, there is little sign of new thinking."

Sustainable economic recovery is not possible until excess capacity is eliminated. Yet despite abysmal prospects, industry refuses to downsize. Over the last decade, industrial Japan added 7.7 percent to its overall manufacturing capacity, even while capacity utilization declined by 16.3 percent.[36] As a result, Japanese industry is estimated to have 85 trillion yen (more than $700 billion) in excess capital stock. In the steel industry, for example, the Japanese market consumes about 80 million metric tons a year. The industry can produce 112 million tons. By comparison, apparent steel consumption in the United States is about 107 million metric tons while production capacity is 108 million metric tons.[37] Both nations' industries have reduced their capacities by about one-fifth from their peak over the last quarter century. But the results are totally different. The United States makes up for shortfalls in meeting domestic demand by importing. Japan, on the other hand, relies on exports to shed itself of the consequences of its continued production over capacity.

[34]"Ghosn's Nissans 'Revival Plan' Is Even Tougher Than Anticipated," *Japan Daily Digest*, Volume X, Number 184, October 19, 1999.

[35]Stephan Strom, "Cuts by Nissan Are Deeper Than Foreseen," *New York Times*, October 19, 1999.

[36]Jesper Koll, "Strategic Investments in Japan: The Economics of Opportunity and the Politics of Obstacles," Jesper Koll Research Paper, January 12, 1999.

[37]Mark Tilton, "Japan's Steel Cartel and the 1998 Steel Export Surge," A Japan Information Access Project Working Paper, October 23, 1998.

Similarly, headline reports of widespread layoffs in Japanese firms artfully mask just how little real personnel restructuring is actually occurring, at least in the short run. Mitsubishi Electric Corporation, for example, announced a total cutback of 14,500 jobs—one-tenth of its total workforce—by fiscal year 2001. On the surface, this would appear to be a significant belt tightening. But of the 8,400 jobs to be lost in Japan, about one-third will come through attrition or slower recruitment. The rest will be achieved through encouraging employees to quit or by selling off subsidiaries. No actual layoffs will occur. One of the touted benefits of the announced merger of the Industrial Bank of Japan, Dai-Ichi Kangyo Bank, and Fuji Bank is that 6,000 jobs will be slashed from a combined payroll of 35,000. But the cuts are to be spread over five years. Nippon Telephone and Telegraph will cut its workforce by 20,000 but in a time span of more than three-and-a-half years. Nissan may have announced unprecedented workforce reductions, but it will all be accomplished through attrition and early retirements. And so it goes down the list of corporate restructurings.[38]

These "headline" layoffs fall short of what is needed to restore Japanese companies to profitability. Japanese corporations now earn only a 2 percent return on their assets. To return to their historical average of 4 percent will require a 10 to 15 percent cut in labor costs.[39]

Moreover, corporate Japan's recent slimming of its labor force pales in comparison to the job cuts made in the United States when American companies were faced with similar competitiveness problems a decade ago. At that time, Ford Motor Company, for instance, slashed its payroll by one-third. And U.S. steelmakers permanently laid off more than 200,000 workers. Overall, American Fortune 500 companies cut 2.8 million employees from their payrolls between 1977 and 1988.[40]

[38] *Business Week International*, September 6, 1999.
[39] Ibid.
[40] Maki Hishikawa, "To Revive the Japanese Economy, Improve the Rule of the Market," *Ekonomisuto*, May 25, 1999, p. 29.

A New Beginning

To date, Japan's jobless rate has more than doubled since the recession began. In 1999, it averaged 4.7 percent, the highest since the government started keeping track in 1953. But by international standards Japan has not nearly begun paying the price of its prolonged economic downturn. In 1991–92, when the United Kingdom last experienced negative growth, the British unemployment rate averaged 9.5 percent. In 1991, when Canada slipped into recession, national unemployment rose higher than 10 percent. And in 1982, during America's most serious recession in recent history, when the GDP shrunk 2.1 percent, U.S. joblessness hit a postwar high of 9.7 percent. The Japanese recession is deeper and more prolonged than any of those downturns were, yet the Japanese unemployment rate in 1999 was 4.7 percent.[41] Japanese economists are quick to argue that their jobless rate would be higher if U.S. measurement standards were applied. But as Douglas Ostrom of the Washington-based Japan Economic Institute has demonstrated, such a recalculation would have raised Japan's average unemployment rate over the last 15 years by a mere three one-hundredths of a percentage point—a distinction without a difference.[42]

Japanese analysts also note that their country's jobless rate would be higher if disguised unemployment were counted. There are an estimated 3 million employees on company books who do no work and whose wages are subsidized by the government. Roughly 30 percent of all industries receive some such aid.[43] Eliminating this public dole would double the national unemployment rate, bringing Japan in line with other industrial nations experiencing deep recessions. But Japan is expanding such aid, not curtailing it—increasing the number of those "employed but not at work," thus inhibiting the process of restructuring.

And despite various workforce initiatives, the Japanese government's approach has been to ride out the recession rather than adapt the workforce to new realities. The government's workforce efforts have

[41]The Council of Economic Advisors, *Economic Report of the President 1999* (Washington, D.C.: U.S. Government Printing Office, February 1999).
[42]Douglas Ostrom, "Unemployment in Japan: How Serious is the Problem?," *JEI Report*, No. 2A, p. 1.
[43]"Japan Selected Issues," IMF.

done little to deal with unwritten lifetime employment guarantees or impediments to layoffs, such as the high cost of shedding workers. And an expanded employment insurance system is not expected to be implemented until March 2001, which gives little solace to workers facing layoffs today.

Corporate Japan has similarly dragged its feet. "It would be a shame [to] think eliminating excess jobs is what structural reform is all about," opined Hiroshi Okuda, Toyota's chair.[44] The Nikkeiren, the Federation of Employers' Associations, echoed such sentiments in January 2000, calling for pay cuts in the name of maintaining employment. Instead of layoffs, most Japanese companies have cut bonuses and hired more part-time workers who do not qualify for the same benefits as full-time employees. Total workers' compensation fell 1.1 percent in 1998, the first such drop in postwar history, and an additional 1.7 percent in 1999.[45] And in 1999 the number of full-time workers was down by 1 percent while the number of part-time workers was up 3.3 percent. As a result, incomes fell 2 percent in 1999.[46]

Curbing labor costs has been a boon to the corporate bottom line. But declining personal income is one of the principal reasons for both Japan's contracting consumer demand and its slide back into recession. And while cutting an employee's wages rather than firing him or her may seem like a humane alternative in the short run, it traps workers, especially younger ones, in dead-end jobs in dying industries, which is hardly in their long-term self-interest or in the interests of their country.

Business restructuring in Japan, much like employment restructuring, has been overhyped. There were nearly 19,000 bankruptcies in 1998 and more than 15,000 in 1999.[47] An impressive total, except that number is still fewer than the business failures expe-

---

[44]"Nissan To Raise Investment $500 Million This Year, Targeting Half at U.S.," *Japan Daily Digest*, Volume XI, Issue 7, January 14, 2000.

[45]Douglas Ostrom, "New Decade, Old Problems," *JEI Report*, No. 8A, February 25, 2000.

[46]Richard Katz, "Reform in Japan: Can the U.S. Help Push the Pace?," *Washington Quarterly*, Autumn 2000.

[47]"Monthly Report of Recent Economic and Financial Developments," Bank of Japan, various issues.

rienced in the early 1980s, suggesting that the Japanese corporate sector made greater adaptations to the last oil crisis than to the current recession, even though economic conditions now are far worse. April 2000 implementation of the Corporate Rehabilitation law should accelerate the pace of restructuring the operations of troubled firms.

Moreover, the volume and value of mergers and acquisitions activity in Japan's corporate sector is impressive only when compared with past Japanese inactivity on that front. In the first half of 1999, the total value of Japanese mergers and acquisitions activity was still equal to only 7 percent of market capitalization in Japan, compared with 14 percent in the United States and 11 percent in the European Union.

The Japanese practice of cross shareholding–in which banks own stock in their borrowers, companies own shares of their lenders, manufacturers own pieces of their suppliers and vice versa—has long warded off undesired acquisitions, especially by foreigners. Recent declines in cross shareholding have been trumpeted as the beginning of the unwinding of Japan, Inc. But such divestitures have merely loosened the knot. The portion of all corporate shares held by a related company was 18.2 percent in 1997 (the latest year for which data is available). A decade earlier, cross shareholding was 21.2 percent, hardly a dramatic shift. More important, the portion of all industrial company stock held by a related company was 14.9 percent in 1997, still greater than the 13.9 percent of cross shareholding in 1987. And in fiscal year 1998, cross shareholding among the big six *keiretsu* was no lower than it was in 1983.[48]

The pace of divestitures will undoubtedly accelerate in the near term. No later than March 2002, each Japanese company will have to declare on its balance sheet the current price of all the shares it holds, rather than value them at their price of acquisition. This could lead some to simply sell off their cross shareholdings because there is no longer any way to mask the decline in the book value

---

[48]Douglas Ostrom, "The Keiretsu System: Cracking or Crumbling?," *JEI Report*, No. 14, April 7, 2000.

of these assets. But until that happens—if it happens—it is premature to say that the interlocking nature of corporate Japan has come to an end.

Japanese resistance to restructuring stems primarily from fear of the pain of transition. Even though the process of economic adjustment is not commonly the topic of international dialogue, because it has been traditionally viewed as a purely domestic concern, Japan's failure to adjust its economy has become a major impediment to the improvement of U.S.-Japan economic relations. For that reason, the United States should press Japan to ease the human suffering caused by layoffs (thus also curtailing the political backlash) and speed restructuring through the following initiatives:

- *Scrap industrial overcapacity.* In previous decades, the Japanese government encouraged the textile and paper industries to shed capacity. It is time to do so again in other industries, but via market pressure rather than through the intervention of the Ministry of International Trade and Industry (MITI). Washington should make it clear to Tokyo that a failure to reduce capacity will self-identify the exports of these industries for closer American scrutiny and possible competition and trade policy initiatives.

- *Make creating a business—and thus creating new jobs—easier.* By MITI's own estimates, the rate of new business formation in Japan is half that in the United States. The creation of a Tokyo Nasdaq should facilitate access to venture capital for small and medium-sized Japanese firms, which will be the main source of jobs for the new Japanese economy. But there is also a need to reduce paperwork and other bureaucratic obstacles to start-up enterprises.

- *Broaden and deepen unemployment compensation.* Current unemployment compensation covers only about 40 percent of the workforce and is insufficiently funded, so it runs out too soon. It is no wonder that there is such political resistance to layoffs. Current plans to improve the safety net are inadequate. Tokyo

A New Beginning

should be encouraged to bring its unemployment compensation more in line with the norm in other industrial nations.

- *Enhance labor mobility.* Japanese workers will oppose restructuring as long as they see job change as a threat, not an opportunity. To create a 21st-century workforce, Japan needs lifelong training and retraining programs.

EXPEDITE DEREGULATION

Deregulation of the Japanese marketplace would arguably do more to spur Japan's economic recovery, open the Japanese economy to foreign competition, and improve U.S.-Japan economic relations than would any other single initiative.

Unfortunately, language is frequently a barrier to communication when Americans and Japanese discuss deregulation. When most Japanese officials speak of deregulation, they do not mean laissez-faire economics. The most commonly used Japanese term in such discussions is *kisei kanwa*, which means to ease or to relax regulations. It does not mean, as many American negotiators have learned to their chagrin, to do away with regulations. Moreover, Japanese and American officials often differ on the implicit purpose of *kisei kanwa.* To Americans, the goal of deregulation is to open the Japanese market to foreign competition. To many Japanese, the object is often to improve competition between Japanese firms in the domestic market in order to enhance Japan's international competitiveness.[49] Such differences in perspective—which may well be rooted in culture but have undeniable real world economic effects—explain the problem, the promise, and the frustration of Japan's deregulatory efforts to date.

Pervasive regulation artificially inflates prices in the Japanese marketplace. A fall 1998 MITI study found that the domestic prices Japanese firms pay for industrial products and services are, on aver-

---

[49]Glen Fukushima, Asahi Evening News, February 5, 1997.

[51]

age, 1.67 times higher than in the United States, 1.57 times higher than in Germany, and 3.3 times higher than in South Korea.[50] Regulations limit store size and location, packaging, and discounting. Japanese consumers now spend 20 percent of their incomes on food—much more than their counterparts in other industrial nations. The cumulative effect of higher prices is stultifying for the economy. Japan is stagnating, not just because people save too much, but because costs are so high that the stimulative effect of any marginal new public or private spending is limited.

In a world where economists seldom agree on anything, there is a rare consensus among the OECD, MITI, and Japan's own Economic Planning Agency (EPA) that deregulation of electricity, air, sea, and ground transportation, telecommunications, and construction would boost Japan's GDP by up to 6 percent.[51] It would achieve such economic benefits, in part, by creating new markets where none existed in the past. In January 1994, for example, there were only 500,000 cell phone subscribers in Japan, thanks in large part to the fact that consumers could only lease phones, not buy them. Liberalization of the cell phone industry led to 24 million being used by June 1997.[52] As experience in the cell phone, large-scale store, and other industries suggests, deregulation of these markets provides great opportunity for American firms to break into the heretofore closed Japanese market.

In the short run, deregulation leads to layoffs. By some estimates, deregulation could lead to the axing of up to 10 percent of the workforce in some industries that now benefit from implicit and explicit price supports. That is a difficult pill to swallow at a time of economic retrenchment. But it is a necessary right of passage toward an economy with a vibrant labor market. The American experience in deregulating telecommunications is illustrative. The U.S. breakup of AT&T cost tens of thousands of workers their jobs. But in 1999, there were

[50]"Japanese Companies Pay Through Nose vs. U.S. Firms, Says MITI Study," *Japan Daily Digest*, Volume X, No. 101, June 7, 1999.
[51]"Japan Selected Issues," IMF.
[52]Richard Katz, *Japan, the System that Soured: The Rise and Fall of the Japanese Economic Miracle* (New York: M.E. Sharpe, Inc., July 1998), p. 20.

more people employed in the U.S. telecommunications sector than before AT&T was dismembered. MITI estimates that deregulation could create 7.4 million jobs by 2010 in the medical care industry, information and telecommunications, distribution, and new manufacturing technologies.

With such benefits to be harvested from deregulation, Tokyo has made limited progress toward a less administered marketplace. Between 1995 and 1997, the Japanese government deregulated 2,823 items (although many of these may have been meaningless). And it has plans to deregulate an additional 627 items. The hotly negotiated and highly controversial deregulation of large-scale retail stores increased the number of such store openings to 2,206 in 1995 from 794 in 1989.[53]

Nevertheless, the Japanese market remains heavily regulated. Deregulation to date has been piecemeal and is rarely accompanied by a meaningful reduction in red tape and other administrative burdens. The government still manages market entry and minimizes market exit, centralizes regulatory authority that could be decentralized, and exercises a high degree of ministerial discretion over economic activity.

The deregulation that has occurred often comes up short, because the goal posts are constantly changing. In 1992, for example, long-distance telephone charges in Japan were higher than those in France, Great Britain, or the United States. In 1998, after extensive telecommunications deregulation, Japanese long-distance costs still remained the highest among major industrial nations. More important, other nations were not standing still. They were also deregulating to boost economic growth. As a result, despite what Tokyo viewed as significant and painful deregulation, Japan found itself losing competitive ground because of its foot-dragging. A 215-mile call in Japan that cost twice as much as a similar call in Britain in 1992 was three times as expensive six years later, even though both calls cost less in absolute numbers.[54]

[53]"Japan Selected Issues," IMF.
[54]"Japan Selected Issues," IMF.

Moreover, planned deregulation may not deliver the benefits advertised. The new large-scale retail store location law is purported to be a deregulatory effort to curtail limits on the opening of discount stores. These outlets are more likely than smaller retailers to carry imported goods. But the new law allows local governments to create special zones for small and medium-sized stores, rules that could impose unreasonable restrictions on retail store locations. Moreover, localities such as Yokohama and Sendai have already used environmental considerations to limit retail store parking and other necessary attributes of large-scale stores.[55] Although some noise and trash limitations are unavoidable, Japan's long history of market resistance to large-scale retailers gives cause for wariness.

To spur greater deregulation of the Japanese economy, Washington should press Tokyo to do the following:

- *Give greater political commitment to deregulation.* Former Prime Minister Hashimoto wanted to be remembered as the "deregulation" prime minister, to little avail. Numerous Japanese business and academic advisory panels have produced reams of deregulation proposals. MITI has self-interestedly nominated itself as the spearhead of deregulation within the Japanese government. The Economic Strategy Council recommended creating a regulatory reform commission, directly reporting to the prime minister, which would be empowered to review regulations, taxation, and subsidies with an eye toward getting government out of the marketplace wherever feasible. The time for study is over—and it is time to produce results.

- *Focus deregulatory efforts on the telecommunications, energy, and transportation sectors.* Industrial electricity rates are currently 33 percent lower in the United States and 19 percent lower in Germany than they are in Japan, according to a MITI study. Railway cargo rates are 39 percent lower in the United States and 33 percent lower in Germany than in Japan. Japanese indus-

[55]"Retail Sales Fell in March, Making a Third Straight Year of Decline," *Japan Daily Digest*, Volume XI, Issue 72, April 27, 2000.

try will be hard pressed to revive itself amid such competitive disadvantages. Moreover, the average Japanese uses the telephone one-third as much as the average American does, in part because the cost of a telephone call is often three times as great. Introducing competition to lower these costs is a necessary precondition for the continued growth of the information technology industry and for the development of electronic commerce in Japan, which would permit new market entrants—both foreign and domestic—to bypass existing archaic distribution systems.

- *Open up the bidding for public works projects to international competition.* Costs of civil engineering projects in Japan are 80 percent higher than in the United States and 60 percent higher than in the European Union. And the closed public works market denies internationally competitive U.S. design and engineering affirms access to the largest construction market in the world.

STRENGTHEN COMPETITION POLICY

Japan has long had a dual economy. One segment of the business arena—including autos, consumer electronics, and machinery—is outward-looking and internationally competitive. A second portion—including steel, construction, and distribution—that sustains and supports the first is still inward-looking, cosseted in exclusionary relationships.

At the core of many U.S. economic problems with Japan is the cartelized nature of this second, inward-looking marketplace. Exclusionary behavior in some major industries, in distribution, and until recently in finance, have proven to be a major impediment to U.S. exports. More important, as U.S. investment in Japan increases and more American companies become players inside the Japanese economy, the nature of competition in that marketplace becomes an ever more significant concern. The recession-driven corporate restructuring now going on in Japan is not sufficient to break some companies' stranglehold on the Japanese economy. Only aggressive enforcement of competition policy laws, including more proactive antitrust actions by the United States, can break these exclusionary practices. Rooting out restrictive business practices—such as price fixing, bid rigging, and market allocation arrangements—has to be the cornerstone of any meaningful restructuring of Japan. Failure to do so will leave the Japanese corporate landscape fundamentally unchanged in its dealings with the rest of the world.

Exclusionary business relationships have a long history in Japan. The prewar economy was dominated by family-led *zaibatsu*—vast holding companies that controlled much economic activity. After the war, these were broken up by American occupation forces. But other exclusionary tie-ups emerged in the form of *keiretsu*: interlocking networks of manufacturers, suppliers, and distributors, some revolving around a particular bank that often served as the main lender for each *keiretsu* group. (In vertical *keiretsu* relationships, an automaker owns a piece of its principal suppliers, who in turn own a piece of it. In horizontal *keiretsu*, companies borrow from the same bank, which also owns stock in its customers.) Then during the 1970s oil crisis, the Japanese government sanctioned the creation of "recession cartels" to sustain troubled industries and maintain employment. These exclusionary impulses persist. To reduce current excess capacity, some Japanese commentators have suggested coordinated capacity cuts—in essence an informal revival of the 1970s recession cartels.

The steel industry is a textbook case of such cozy relationships, oligopoly market sharing, and similar exclusionary practices in the Japanese economy. Market shares for domestic steelmakers have been stable since 1973, hardly the sign of vibrant competition. Such implicit collusion has permitted Japan's five major integrated steel producers to charge domestic prices that are about twice as high as world market prices for sales that make up about two-fifths of the Japanese market. Such price differentials would not be sustainable in the face of unfettered international competition. So it comes as no surprise that imports account for only 7 percent of Japanese consumption (imports account for 25 percent of U.S. consumption).[56] Such exclusionary practices have exacted a heavy toll from Japanese consumers and the Japanese economy. Retail prices may be as much as 40 percent higher, thanks to restrictive business behavior.

The United States has also paid a price. Although the surge in U.S. steel imports from Japan in 1998 is attributable to many factors, Japan would not have been in a position to ratchet up exports so dramatically without the existence of excess capacity in its industry. (At the time, production was 40 percent above domestic demand.) And this excess capacity was only sustainable through the continuation of the informal steel cartel, the limitation of steel imports, regulatory barriers to steelmakers exiting the industry, and investors' utter disregard for steelmakers return on capital. More broadly, Japan's limited consumption of imported manufactured goods and its small amount of FDI are the price the whole world pays for Japan's exclusionary domestic marketplace.

The Japan Fair Trade Commission (JFTC) is charged with ensuring a competitive market in Japan. But the JFTC is clearly not up to the task. In postwar history, the government has brought only a handful of cases under the Japan Anti-Monopoly Law.

Shortcomings in quantity are not compensated for by the quality of JFTC cases. At the same time when the U.S. Department of Justice was busy prosecuting Microsoft, one of the world's largest companies, the JFTC was demonstrating its newfound activism by going after Japan's leading maker of residential area maps. Moreover, JFTC actions often impede rather than promote competition. In fiscal year 1999, the JFTC issued 672 administrative warnings against companies selling products at an "unfair" discount, 429 of these against liquor stores that dared to sell cheap beer.

Such government inaction would be lamentable, but tolerable, if private citizens in Japan could enforce competition laws themselves. But since 1955, only 15 private antitrust cases have been filed and not one has been won. (In the United States, by comparison,

[56]Mark Tilton, "Japan's Steel Cartel and the 1998 Steel Export Surge," A Japan Information Access Project Working Paper, October 23, 1998.

since the Sherman Antitrust Act was passed, there were more than 26,000 private antitrust cases.)[57]

For a number of years, the U.S. government has attempted through both the Structural Impediments Initiative with Japan and the Framework talks to prompt greater JFTC activism. But success has been elusive. American pressure led to increases in the JFTC budget and personnel, some increase in enforcement actions, and greater penalties in some cases. But it did little to change the agency's "hear no evil, see no evil" view of the Japanese business landscape. A case in point is the JFTC's treatment of Japan's flat glass market, which is tightly controlled by three companies. Under pressure from the United States, the JFTC agreed to study the flat glass industry. But a May 1999 study found no anticompetitive practices, a finding that belies the 2 percent share of the market held by American producers—far smaller than their share in other countries.

On a separate track, the U.S. Justice Department has attempted to increase cooperation and dialogue with the JFTC and has negotiated a positive comity agreement between Washington and Tokyo. Under this compact, if the Justice Department has reason to believe that corporate practices in Japan are damaging U.S. companies or consumers, it can ask JFTC to investigate and vice versa. It is too soon to know how well the agreement will work. But the International Competition Policy Advisory Committee to the U.S. Justice Department concluded in its February 2000 report that, "The historic enforcement record of antitrust agencies around the world does not instill confidence in those agencies' willingness to pursue antitrust actions against domestic firms in instances where the practices of those firms have allegedly impaired the ability of foreign firms to compete effectively." There is a need to build more structure into transpacific antitrust cooperation. Experience suggests this will not happen through Japanese initiative. It can only be the product of U.S. pressure for change, when conflict is the alternative to cooperation.

Responsibility for the failure to enforce antitrust law rests, however, on both sides of the Pacific. During the Bush adminis-

---

[57]Maki Hishikawa, "To Revive the Japanese Economy, Improve the Rule of the Market," *Ekonomisuto*, May 25, 1999, p. 29.

tration, the Justice Department asserted it would take action against foreign restraints on U.S. exports if such conduct was having a "direct, substantial and reasonably foreseeable effect" on the ability of American firms to sell in a foreign market. To its credit, the Justice Department subsequently worked with the JFTC to open the Japanese soda-ash market. But the Justice Department under Bush and Clinton never brought a case to open a foreign market for U.S. exports of manufactured products.[58]

This failing highlights the limitation of the current American approach to antitrust issues with Japan. Competition policy in the United States is largely under the purview of antitrust lawyers in the Justice Department and the Federal Trade Commission (FTC). Trade policy is the preserve of trade negotiators at United States Trade Representative (USTR). These are different professional communities with dissimilar world views, subject to separate political pressures and often pursuing divergent objectives.

Antitrust lawyers have traditionally worried about the domestic U.S. market. They have scrutinized foreign anticompetitive behavior only when it affected prices and competition in the American market. Trade negotiators worry about market restraints abroad that impede U.S. exports and investment. Moreover, competition policy experts tend to evaluate business collusion in terms of its effect on consumer welfare. Trade policy experts evaluate whether or not a producer is being kept out of a market unfairly by virtue of some restraint, even if that restraint may benefit consumers in the foreign market. Competition policy is often caste as a high-minded pursuit of economic efficiency. Trade policy is often little more than the handmaiden of individual U.S. firms with a grievance abroad. Most important from a political point of view, efforts to apply U.S. antitrust policy in foreign markets and to spur exports and American investment have been shackled by the U.S. companies fears that an activist U.S. competition policy abroad would

---

[58]Merit E. Janow, "A Look at U.S.-EU Cooperation in Competition Policy," *Competition Policy in the European Union and the United States* (Washington, D.C.: Brookings Institution, forthcoming).

lead foreigners to challenge allegedly anticompetitive U.S. corporate practices that are now tolerated in the American market.

This deadlock between a trade policy and a competition policy view of the world was tolerable when exports and overseas investment were relatively less important to the welfare of the domestic U.S. economy. It was tolerable when Tokyo maintained significant tariffs, and when its exclusionary business practices were of secondary importance to American commercial success in the Japanese marketplace. It was acceptable when there was little prospect of U.S. companies setting up shop inside the Japanese market, and attempting to do business there. That world has now changed, however, and it is time for the United States to develop a coherent and mutually reinforcing trade and competition policy toward Japan that focuses on market opening and a truly competitive domestic market for foreigners who invest there.

Such an effort will face practical obstacles. U.S. courts and the U.S. Justice Department have no power to compel foreign firms to produce evidence. Moreover, such an initiative will undoubtedly be resisted in Japan. Tokyo will complain about the extraterritorial application of U.S. law. But a signal must be sent that the United States is no longer willing to look the other way when exclusionary practices deny American firms access to the second-largest market in the world, and that it will not tolerate implicit discrimination against American investors in Japan. In the long run, the only way to achieve a Japanese marketplace that is truly open to foreign competition is through a more active and effective JFTC. But more than a decade of prodding the JFTC has produced scant results. It is time for the United States to force the action. Such efforts will be fiercely resented in Japan, but experience suggests that unilateral initiatives are often the only way to break a logjam. (It was U.S. trade cases brought against music and video piracy that finally forced the world community to take intellectual property protection seriously.)

At the same time, such an effort will cause a firestorm of criticism from antitrust lawyers in the United States, who will resent the intrusion of trade lawyers onto their turf. So be it. There is a need in Washington to break the stalemate between the USTR and the Justice Department on the application of antitrust policy abroad. In the spirit that competition breeds creative solutions to problems, new actors—such as the USTR, the Commerce Department, and the Federal Trade Commission—must be brought into the policy mix as the United States wrestles with exclusionary practices in Japan.

To encourage a more competitive domestic Japanese marketplace, the United States should do the following:

* *Publish an annual review of Japanese exclusionary practices.* This study, as part of the yearly National Trade Estimates report, should include an assessment of their impact on U.S. industry and workers. The assessment could identify cases of significant price differentials for the same good or service to highlight possible exclusionary practices.

* *File antitrust cases against Japanese conduct that impedes U.S. exports.* It has long been U.S. policy that the United States has the power to do this. It should exercise that prerogative.

* *Launch FTC investigations of exclusionary Japanese activities that burden U.S. commerce.* The Justice Department argues that it cannot bring antitrust cases because it lacks the power to gather evidence in Japan. To overcome this problem, the president's Commission on United States-Pacific Trade and Investment Policy recommended legislation directing the FTC to investigate claims of anticompetitive practices in cases when evidence proved impossible to gather and, where appropriate, simply to issue cease and desist orders and impose fines.

* *Press Tokyo to enforce its antitrust law meaningfully.* Legal changes are needed in Japan to facilitate the filing of private antitrust suits. The JFTC staff is too small and the bureaucracy too much under the thumb of the Ministry of Finance. Despite a recommendation by the Economic Strategy Council that "the Fair Trade Commission needs to be dramatically strengthened by reorganizing its structure and by increasing the number of its secretariat to secure judicial independence," the fiscal year

1999 JFTC budget gave the agency only nine additional staff members.

- *Hire a prominent antitrust lawyer as special counsel to USTR to provide impetus and stature for a more proactive, market-opening antitrust policy.*

REFORM CORPORATE GOVERNANCE

Corporate governance reform is a necessary driver of economic restructuring in Japan. Changes in management practices will not eliminate all the shortcomings of Japanese-style capitalism, nor will they necessarily reduce the U.S.-Japan trade imbalance. Nonetheless, corporate reform promises manifold benefits for the bilateral economic relationship: it is market-oriented, has a strong domestic constituency in Japan, does not enhance the power of Tokyo bureaucrats, and does not require tedious sessions of trade negotiations. More specifically, corporate governance reform will force Japanese firms to focus more intently on the return on equity, which in turn will undermine import-restricting exclusionary business practices, make it easier for foreigners to acquire local sales and service firms, and inhibit predatory export pricing by Japanese firms by making the expansion of productive capacity more sensitive to the true cost of capital.

In some quarters in Tokyo these recommendations will be resisted as an American attempt to impose its standards on a Japanese business community with a long-ingrained and, until recently, a highly successful business culture of its own. There was similar American resistance to the adoption of some Japanese management practices in the 1980s. But just as the U.S. corporate community was eventually forced by competitive pressures to adapt, it is now time for Japan's business leadership to change ways. With international capital and management personnel increasingly able to migrate to the best-run, most successful firms—whatever their national origin—Japanese corporations must change their ways in order to compete successfully with American and European firms.

A New Beginning

Economic globalization requires global business standards. Obviously one size does not fit all, but converging on a set of "global best practices" is probably inevitable. U.S. corporate governance practices have, in many cases, become de facto global standards, not because they are American but because in many business sectors U.S. firms have been the first to organize themselves as truly global companies that are forced to compete for capital on a worldwide basis. Thus, good governance is not a question of the Americanization of Japanese business practices. Rather, it is an issue of the globalization of Japanese business practices. If Japan were almost any other country, the world would not care if Japanese firms ran themselves according to global standards or local custom. But Japanese corporations do not have that luxury. How Japanese corporations govern themselves directly affects Japan's potential for economic recovery and the competitive nature of Japan's domestic market, both vital interests of the United States, Europe, and the rest of Asia.

One explanation for Japan's poor economic performance over the last decade is Japanese management's dismal performance in the use of capital. From 1989 to 1996, among Japan's top 300 nonfinancial companies, the annual average return on investment—after accounting for the cost of both debt and equity capital—was negative 1.8 percent. By comparison, the annual average return for the American industrial firms followed by Standard & Poors was a positive 1 percent.[59]

During the 1980s bubble economy, a rising tide appeared to lift all boats, obscuring the fact that many Japanese firms were losing money. The recent recession focused the harsh light of day on these losses and the slack corporate governance practices that permitted them.

Corporate boards in Japan are largely made up of managers. Only one-quarter of Japanese public firms have an outside director, and even these generally represent the interests of the company's main bank or an affiliated firm. Even the statutory auditor, nominally

---

[59]James Shinn, "Corporate Governance Reform and Trade Friction," A CFR study group working paper, March 1999.

independent, is usually a former employee. Experience demonstrates that these insiders resist accountability and change even in the face of persistently poor management performance. And given Japan's spotty accounting standards, even conscientious boards can never be quite certain how the firm is doing.

With crony supervision and inadequate information, it is little wonder that Japanese companies have been insensitive to the return on equity, slow to downsize, reluctant to divest themselves of cross shareholdings, and generally resistant to the kinds of changes that would help create a new, more sustainable Japanese economy—one that is more open to global competition.

But these are structural problems, not cultural differences, and they can be solved by structural management changes (which admittedly will entail painful dislocations within Japanese firms). The management changes begun at Nissan and other Japanese firms that now have foreign participation and the reforms slowly taking place as *keiretsu* unwind demonstrate that Japanese corporate culture can adapt.

Because a growing number of Japanese companies do business and raise capital in the United States, Washington has far more leverage over Japanese corporate governance practices than might seem apparent at first. Exercising that leverage would be a significant departure in U.S.-Japan relations, but few initiatives promise as much payoff.

To that end, Washington should do the following:

- *Hold Japanese issuers of securities to the same standards of good governance that apply to U.S. and other international borrowers.* These standards include the use of independent external auditors (a proposal that has the backing of Keidanren) and an audit committee of the board with a majority of outside directors (Sony has outside directors, so others can too).

- *Scrutinize the governance standards of the Japanese banks and security firms that are licensed to operate in the U.S. financial market and deny them the right to do business if their substandard governance practices pose a danger to U.S. financial markets.*

- *Bring Japanese accounting practices in line with "global best practice."* Such a move has the support of Japan's Business Accounting Deliberation Council. Encourage the "Big Five" global accounting firms to conduct a formal review to insure that their Japanese affiliates adhere to global standards of rigor and disclosure.

ENCOURAGE FOREIGN DIRECT INVESTMENT

Japan's recession has opened the door to foreign investment. Rock-bottom asset prices and the need for injections of capital have created unprecedented investment opportunities. As a major investor in Japan, the United States is in the best position to exploit these opportunities.

The financial sector was the first to open to foreign funds, in part due to Japan's Big Bang reforms, but largely thanks to financial institutions' enormous debt burden that left them little choice but to sell themselves to the highest bidder. In July 1998, Merrill Lynch took over Yamaichi Securities, creating Merrill Lynch Japan Securities Company, the only foreign company selling stocks, bonds, and mutual funds directly to individual Japanese investors. Travelers Group has a 25 percent share of Nikko Securities. Salomon Smith Barney and Morgan Stanley Japan now have all acquired brokerage businesses in Tokyo. And the nationalized Long-Term Credit Bank has been sold to the American firm Ripplewood Holdings.

This invasion may transform the delivery of financial services in Japan. Foreign brokerages now manage more than one-third of the total trading volume on the Tokyo Stock Exchange. About 10 percent of the outstanding balance of Japanese trust funds is now managed by foreigners. Since the process of managing pension monies was open to foreigners in 1990, an estimated one-third to one-half has been put in the hands of foreigners.[60]

---

[60]"Japan's Securities Industry: From Big Bank to E-Boom," *JEI Report*, No. 22A, June 11, 1999, p. 10.

Foreign financial firms have facilitated the movement of foreign capital into the Tokyo securities market. Foreigners accounted for more than 40 percent of the total value of shares traded in Japan in 1998, up from 12 percent in 1990. And foreigners now own about 10 percent of all shares of listed companies in Japan, up from 4.2 percent in 1990.

Foreign investment fever has also spread to the manufacturing sector. Seven of Japan's nine car and light truck builders now have partial foreign ownership. German auto parts giant Robert Bosch has control of Japanese fuel injection specialist Zexel. Goodyear has acquired 10 percent of Sumitomo Rubber, creating the world's largest tire combine.

As encouraging as these signs are, it is still too early to judge their significance. There have been foreign investment booms in the past, such as in the nineteenth century during the Meiji era and again after World War II. This recent wave of foreign investment is simply bottom-feeding. In 1998 and 1999, four-fifths of merger and acquisition deals in Japan by foreigners involved distressed companies, according to a study by Bain & Company. This reflects a fleeting opening to the world at a time when the economy has no other choice.

Moreover, troubling reminders of Japan's resistance to foreign investment remain. In early 2000, nationalist opposition in the Diet blocked the sale of Nippon Credit Bank to the U.S.-based Cerebrus Group, leading to its purchase by a consortium led by Japan's Softbank. This xenophobia cost Japanese taxpayers $540 million, the difference between Softbank's purchase price and Cerebrus' offer.[61]

To ensure that Japan's door to foreign investment remains open and to build on recent foreign investment successes in Japan, the U.S. government should encourage Japan to enhance the climate for foreign investment through further deregulation, reform of land-use policies to open up land for investment, tax changes,

---

[61]"Nationalism Allowed Softbank To Buy NCB for Yen 60 Billion Less Than Cerebrus Bid," *Japan Daily Digest*, Volume XI, Issue 34, February 28, 2000.

vigorous enforcement of antitrust law and greater transparency in government procedures and corporate financial dealings.

The following recommendations concern what Tokyo can do to help itself and, by extension, the United States and Japan's other global economic partners. Ultimately, such reforms are beyond Washington's control. On its own initiative, the new American administration and U.S. Congress should also pursue a number of policies, described later.

A PROACTIVE TRADE POLICY

Over the years, the United States has pursued a variety of approaches to open the Japanese market and resolve trade disputes with Japan. There have been one-off negotiations, such as the 1986 Semiconductor Agreement. To create a sense of momentum and urgency, there have been multi-issue negotiations, such as the Market Oriented Sector Selective (MOSS) talks from 1985 to 1986, which included negotiations on electronics and telecommunications products, pharmaceuticals and medical equipment, and forest products. Beginning in 1989, there was the Structural Impediments Initiative (SII), intended "to identify and solve structural problems in both countries which stand as impediments to trade," such as Japan's Large-Scale Retail Store Law and Tokyo's failure to vigorously pursue antitrust cases. The Clinton administration updated the SII, first with the Framework talks and then with a deregulation initiative.

Such efforts have produced some notable successes. The 1986 U.S.-Japan Semiconductor Agreement, including the subsequent updatings of that pact, is probably the single most successful American trade agreement with Japan. Since that deal was struck, the U.S. share of the Japanese semiconductor market has grown from one-twelfth to one-third. The 1994 cellular phone agreement led to an explosion in cell phone use in Japan. And the 1995 auto parts agreement has significantly increased sales of U.S.-made parts in Japan.[62]

But of fifty-one U.S. trade agreements with Japan since 1980, only twenty-seven can be termed fully or mostly successful. Another nine were partly successful. And fifteen only were successful in one or two ways or were completely unsuccessful, according to an assessment by the American Chamber of Commerce in Japan.

---

[62]*Making Trade Talks Work*, American Chamber of Commerce in Japan (New York: Charles E. Tuttle Co., Inc., 1999).

A .529 batting average would be phenomenal in baseball, but it will not get many trade negotiators into the Hall of Fame.

Broad lessons can be drawn from these experiences:

- *Leverage helps.* Japanese semiconductor makers faced prohibitive U.S. duties if they failed to open their domestic market to foreign competition, thus helping convince them to accede to the Semiconductor Agreement.

- *Its easier to push on an open door.* In the early 1990s, Japan realized it had to update its intellectual property laws for the sake of its own industry, and therefore, it could be convinced to change the way it treated sound recordings and patents.

- *It pays to be specific.* MOSS and SII both produced agreements with so much wiggle room that results were frequently hard to measure.

- *Short time frames lead to truncated results.* Japanese negotiators have learned to wait out their American counterparts, knowing that the U.S. desire for quick fixes will lead Washington to accept suboptimal solutions.

- *Fragmentation within the U.S. government has frequently been Japan's most powerful ally.* All too often, one segment of the U.S. government has undercut another. As a result U.S. goals have frequently been dramatically watered down, even before negotiations ever began.

LIMITED UNILATERAL REMEDIES

The United States has limited unilateral remedies to improve its track record for dealing with disputes with Japan or other trading partners.

The antidumping law has been employed recently in response to the dramatic increase in Japanese steel shipments to the United States. Shipments subsequently subsided, thanks to the threat or imposition of duties (according to the U.S. industry) or because U.S. demand subsided (according to the Japanese industry).

Antidumping duties remain the single most potent trade tool available to United States, but their use is necessarily limited. Duties can only be imposed on a narrow universe of imports that can be proven to injure, or threaten to injure, U.S. firms when they are sold at less than fair value. There is a growing domestic constituency that depends on imports and is opposed to the antidumping statutes because they interfere with markets, distort prices, and encourage rent-seeking behavior by domestic firms. And although dumping duties close down the U.S. market to imports, they generally do nothing to open foreign markets. As a result, dumping duties are on the endangered species list.

Section 301 of the 1974 Trade Act allows the USTR to impose duties on imports from countries trading unfairly, including a closed market to U.S. products. But there have been no Section 301 cases filed since completion of the Uruguay Round, because the United States bound itself to take such disputes to the WTO. This neutering of Section 301 has severely constrained U.S. bilateral leverage with Japan. The United States could, however, still bring a Section 301 case against Japan if it is willing to pay compensation for that action.

Section 201 of the Trade Act allows an injured industry temporary relief when imports surge. And imports from Japan, among those from other countries, have been the subject of two recent Section 201 cases. However, the Clinton administration dragged its feet in deciding the cases. And the Section 201 option suffers the same shortcoming as the antidumping laws in that it protects the U.S. market but does not necessarily work to open a foreign market.

Finally, various administrative options are available to increase leverage on Japan, or other trading partners, and send a signal of U.S. concern. During the auto dispute in the early days of the Clinton administration there was some discussion of imposing the same rigorous inspection standards on imported Japanese cars that Japan then imposed on foreign autos. But nothing came of this proposal. In 1997, the Federal Maritime Commission (FMC) threatened to close U.S. ports to Japanese ships unless Japan reformed its protectionist port practices. The move engendered quick promises of reform from Tokyo. And though American firms still lack the ability to set up their own port operations, the FMC action highlighted Japan's vulnerability to targeted initiatives based on administrative discretion.

Opponents of such administrative harassment argue that great nations do not stoop to such tactics, that in America's litigious society any bureaucrat attempting such discretionary action would immediately be enjoined with a law suit, and that the only reason the FMC got as far as it did was because it is an independent agency and did not have to clear its action with the White House.

ENCOURAGING MULTILATERAL OPTIONS

The U.S. track record in resolving its economic problems with Japan through multilateral means is encouraging but limited. The United States has brought eight WTO cases against Japan. Six have been victorious, including a success in February 1999 in which a WTO dispute panel found that Japan acted illegally by blocking imports of such fruits as apples and cherries.

The major U.S. loss came in the Kodak-Fuji dispute, in which the WTO denied U.S. complaints that Japanese government administrative guidance had promoted exclusionary behavior in the Japanese market for consumer color film. The Kodak judgment set a high threshold for evaluating the evidence needed to prove restrictive government-industry behavior, a key issue in any future U.S. dispute with Japan. The outcome suggests that successful WTO cases against Japanese market barriers will require relatively simple and straightforward cases involving proof of written government directives closing the Japanese market.

To pursue a more proactive trade policy toward Japan, the United States should:

- *Face Japan united.* The highest priority for crafting a successful Japan trade policy is consensus at home. Such unity flows from the top. There is no substitute for presidential leadership. In the first two years of the Clinton administration, U.S.

trade policy toward Japan was remarkably coherent because of presidential engagement. Future policy will require similar Oval Office involvement.

- *Accept that there is no silver bullet in dealing with Japan.* Both sector-specific and structural negotiations are likely to be necessary in the future as U.S. trade officials slog it out in trench warfare on a necessarily narrow range of American market access concerns.

- *Reinvigorate unilateral trade options.* Unilateralism provides Washington with its most useful leverage in its bilateral dealings with Tokyo. It provides leverage in seeking multilateral solutions to trade problems. It is tangible evidence to skeptical domestic audiences that an administration is willing to stand up for U.S. self-interest. Where appropriate, one or more Section 301 cases should be brought against Japan in areas not adequately covered now by the WTO—such as government procurement—to reassert this trade policy option and encourage Tokyo to consider broadening its multilateral disciplines in these areas. To augment the WTO and legal tools available to the United States, Section 201 should be made easier to use and relief should be more automatic.

- *Do not rule out administrative options.* Former Secretary of State Henry Kissinger has championed the value of a small dose of irrationality in the conduct of foreign policy. Trade policy toward Japan would benefit from a similar unpredictability. An occasional decision by the U.S. Customs Service or a regulatory agency to "work to rule" with regard to a particular import from Japan would signal Washington's seriousness to Tokyo. A list of potential administrative leverage points with Japan should be compiled, and the president's authority to engage in reciprocal trade actions should be enhanced.

- *Pursue a full agenda of WTO cases.* Tokyo has scored diplomatic points by portraying itself as the defender of multilateralism against the unilateralist proclivities of the United States. Washington should call Tokyo's bluff and seize every opportunity to face off against Japan in Geneva at the WTO. Experience suggests that the United States has a good chance of winning those cases. Even when it loses, Washington will expose Tokyo's economic practices for the world to scrutinize and will further clarify the limitations of the WTO system. And Japan will frequently prefer to resolve disputes bilaterally, as it did in 1997 when a threatened U.S. WTO case on telecommunications procurement led to a settlement.

- *Link bilateral goals with Japan to multilateral objectives.* More transparent public procurement and more liberal rules for electronic commerce are high on the U.S. agenda with Japan and are also U.S. goals for any new multilateral trade negotiations. Washington should make it clear to Tokyo that if there is no multilateral progress on these issues, it will aggressively pursue them bilaterally.

- *Trust but verify.* A proactive economic policy with Japan requires people and money. The Commerce Department's Market Access and Compliance Unit, which monitors the implementation of U.S. trade agreements, had seventeen people working on Japan issues in 1992. In 2000, it had nine. The USTR often has one Japanese speaker on staff. An increase in personnel and resources is long overdue.

EUROPE AS A PARTNER

Future U.S. trade policy toward Japan stands a much better chance of succeeding if, whenever possible, Washington coordinates its efforts with Brussels. As the other major global economy, the European Union (EU) has much to gain from a Japan that is more open to trade and foreign investment and more willing to play by accepted multilateral rules when exporting. And it has a great deal to lose if it allows Tokyo to play itself off against Washington.

Over many years, the EU and the United States worked at cross purposes in dealing with Japan. Brussels opposed the U.S.-Japan

Semiconductor Agreement and yet wanted to be part of it once it succeeded. Europeans chastised Americans for their heavy-handed effort to increase U.S. market share in the Japanese auto sector. For their part, Americans were mystified by European acceptance of their own small sliver of the Japanese market.

This failure to cooperate largely reflected differences in economic self-interest. Europe was not sufficiently competitive in semiconductors, super computers, agricultural products, and other topics of U.S.-Japan trade negotiations to take advantage of any market opening that might ensue. But this divergence of interests has now begun to change. The German filmmaker Agfa joined Kodak in its groundbreaking WTO case against Fuji. Washington joined Brussels in its case against Tokyo's excise taxes on imported liquor. Moreover, experience suggests that in defending themselves against Japanese exports—recall the recent U.S. steel antidumping case and the EU's ongoing quota on imports of Japanese cars—Europe and America risk inadvertently hurting each other through trade diversion. Thus a convergence of self-interest has created opportunities for unprecedented cooperation in dealing with Japan.

To that end, the U.S. government should: develop a priority list of WTO cases for the EU and the United States jointly to file against Japan; invite the EU to join the current U.S. deregulation initiative with Japan and propose efforts to encourage Japan's economic restructuring; consult Brussels before taking unilateral trade actions, whether they be antitrust proceedings, efforts to open the Japanese market, or antidumping cases. Such consultation could, where appropriate, lead to joint action.

AN INFORMATION-BASED TRADE POLICY

In the 21st century, fewer and fewer trade negotiations will focus on tangible external barriers, such as tariffs. They will increasingly involve detailed discussion of intangible, domestic practices, such as regulatory activities. These trade policy challenges will place a growing premium on in depth studies and up-to-the minute assessments of emerging trade and investment conditions. Whatever the U.S. trade policy toward Japan, it will not succeed without a better capacity to gather and analyze information concerning Japanese market conditions and economic policy developments.

Moreover, U.S. trade policy toward Japan has frequently been criticized for being industry driven. This problem is only likely to worsen. As trade cases become increasingly information intensive—relying on a detailed understanding of how a distribution network functions or how an amendment to an obscure regulation might affect a market—only business has this information or the vested interest and resources to develop it. To insure that future trade cases are driven by national interest rather than by the priorities of "squeaky wheel" companies, the U.S. government needs an independent analytical capacity to build future trade cases. The personnel skills needed for this task obviously include superior Japanese language training and a deep understanding of Japanese culture and politics. But they also go beyond traditional trade negotiating talents to include greater expertise in finance, science, and technology.

The United States will pay a high price for its lack of independent, high-quality information and analysis concerning market access and business conditions in Japan. The Kodak brief submitted in its WTO case against Fuji was the most comprehensive assessment of a particular market access problem in Japan that had ever been assembled; and it cost millions of dollars to prepare. The fact that Kodak lost the case makes it unlikely that any company will ever again spend that kind of time and money in building a case against Japan. And the USTR does not have the resources to mount a similar analytical effort on other issues in the future.

In fact, Washington does not even have the capacity to keep up with legislative and regulatory developments in Tokyo that might affect economic interests. In 1995, the Japanese Diet passed a "Law to Promote Business Reform of Special Industries." Under that measure, industries can collude to prepare a business reform plan, qualifying for tax breaks, low interest loans, and subsidies. Even though Washington was engaging in the Framework talks

Stokes

with Tokyo at the time, no one in the U.S. government was aware of the existence of that law.[63]

In order to insure a solid information base for Washington's future trade strategy with regard to Tokyo, the U.S. government needs an enhanced information and analytical capacity. To this effect, the U.S. government should:

- *Station an assistant U.S. Trade Representative in Tokyo.* The USTR has long had an office in Brussels. American market access problems in Japan should be given no less attention.

- *Beef up the Tokyo embassy's economic information gathering and analytical capacity.* With the growing amount of U.S. investment in Japan, the U.S. government needs its own understanding of the "inside-the-castle" problems such investors are encountering.

- *Create a Japan analysis unit in the U.S. Commerce Department or at the International Trade Commission (ITC) solely dedicated to assessing market conditions in Japan for use in market-opening, competition policy, and deregulation initiatives.* This public capacity would free the USTR from a reliance on self-interested industry analysis and permit greater choice in picking its trade cases, rather than frequently relying on whatever information comes in over the transom.

- *Alternatively, contract out such analytical work to private sector consultants under a trust fund controlled by the USTR.* The money for this effort could come either from fines and duties collected in the cases won through such analysis or from double-blind corporate donations.

---

[63]Charles D. Lake II, private communication, December 15, 1999.

CONGRESS AS TRADE OMBUDSMAN

Congress has for too long neglected its vital role in trade policy, especially with regard to Japan. Congress must reassert its capacity as a trade ombudsman, a sounding board for complaints, a promoter of new policy initiatives, and an active partner with the executive branch in shaping U.S. trade relations with the rest of the world.

The U.S. Constitution gives Congress the final authority over trade policy. After asserting this prerogative during the 1980s, pressing the Reagan administration to take the rising trade deficit more seriously and proactively attack market access problems abroad, Congress has become more passive on trade in recent years.

This trend runs counter to underlying changes in the U.S. economy. As trade and investment with Japan and the rest of the world grow in importance—not only to Wall Street but also to Main Street—the elected representatives of those interests will increasingly want to make their voices heard on policies that increasingly affect their constituents.

Moreover, the lesson of the 1980s is that Congressional activism on trade pays dividends. The Reagan administration's 1985 about-face on the exchange rate and the subsequent Plaza Accord that doubled the yen's value might never have happened if Congress had not been pressing for some action on the bilateral trade imbalance. The SII negotiations were a direct consequence of Congressional demands for the USTR to go after Japanese structural impediments to trade. And most significantly, an activist Congress enabled the USTR to play the good cop while Congress was the bad cop in its dealing with Tokyo. The threat of a "protectionist" Congress run amok was useful bargaining leverage in extracting concessions from Japan.

Of course, there are limits to Congress' trade role. The United States cannot have 535 trade negotiators. Congress can push for a change of course in trade policy, but it will only complicate matters if it attempts to dictate the details of a trade deal. As befits a representative democracy, individual members of Congress—in their efforts to effectively speak for the interests of industries in their districts—will frequently advocate policies of narrow and often protectionist self-interest, rather than outward looking policies with a broader national self-interest. It remains the responsibility of the executive branch to speak for the national economy as a whole and to counterbalance particularistic voices on Capitol Hill.

At the same time, experience in the 1990s suggests there are also practical limits on the executive branch's trade policy activism, especially toward Japan. The Clinton administration took office determined to adopt a tougher line toward Japan than its predecessors took. And it did so. But the June 1995 confrontation with Tokyo over access to Japan's auto market demonstrated the constraints on the White House's range of options in such circumstances. Fear of destabilizing financial markets led the administration to strike a deal with Tokyo rather than impose sanctions on Japan that would have led to a WTO case with a questionable outcome.

Congress is needed therefore as a necessary counterbalance to the Treasury, State, and Defense Departments' demands to ease trade pressure on Tokyo—especially since each has its own non-trade agenda with Japan. Only if Congress takes on this ombudsman role can an effective system of checks and balances on trade policy be established for the future. Recent strong support for steel quotas on Capitol Hill suggests renewed Congressional interest in trade policy. But just as American self-interest in economic relations with Japan has grown from purely trade issues to encompass banking concerns, electronic commerce, competition policy, and a host of other issues, the number of Congressional stakeholders in U.S. Japan policy must extend beyond those traditionally found in the Senate Finance Committee and the House Ways and Means Committee. This reborn activism can best be shaped and steered in a positive direction by regular oversight hearings on the U.S.-Japan economic relationship by a range of Congressional committees, and by periodic Congressional initiatives to force administration action on longstanding U.S. economic concerns with Japan.

A New Beginning

TALK SOFTLY, CARRY A BIG STICK

Washington has long labored under the self-delusion that it can force Tokyo to move in directions the Japanese do not want to go. *Gaiatsu*, or foreign pressure, will never succeed in transforming Japan into an American-style economy. But it can help Japan reform its marketplace to an extent acceptable to the Japanese people. And *gaiatsu* can clearly delineate for the Japanese the costs of their continued failure to adapt to a more market-oriented, open economy.

Washington has repeatedly applied pressure on Tokyo to resolve a host of trade and economic policy disputes that have ranged from the ridiculous, an inability to sell American baseball bats in Japan, to the sublime, the value of the yen. Japanese officials have frequently encouraged *gaiatsu* in private discussions with Americans as a means of using external pressure to break an internal policy deadlock in Tokyo.

But in recent years, a game that had become formulaic—an initial Japanese refusal to consider changing its ways, followed by mounting U.S. pressure marked by harsh rhetoric and threats of sanctions, and then ending with a begrudging Japanese reform—turned sour. Tokyo initially refused to even discuss with Washington Kodak's allegations of a closed Japanese market for photographic film. Officials in Tokyo reacted bitterly to initial pressure from the U.S. Treasury to increase government spending and bail out debt-ridden Japanese banks.

This increasingly outspoken resistance to *gaiatsu* is a potentially dangerous development in U.S.-Japan relations. Japan is, after all, a proud, sovereign nation with a history of nationalism and a small but vocal minority seeking to exploit Japanese frustration with U.S. criticism. And the backlash against *gaiatsu* has never been worse, according to a number of Japan scholars. Obviously, a revival of anti-Americanism would not serve U.S. interests. And any U.S. attempt to pressure Japan to change its economic policies must be tempered by a sensitivity to the nationalist undercurrent in Japanese society.

But such awareness need not hobble Washington's pursuit of America's economic self-interest. The Japanese market is too important to the world and to the United States to allow Japanese nationalist sensibilities to predetermine the nature of Tokyo's economic and political dialogue with its trading partners. Japan must realize that a price of deriving the benefits of globalization is an acceptance that its once purely domestic concerns are now open to international scrutiny.

The confrontation with this harsh reality may explain the vehemence with which Japan currently rejects *gaiatsu*. Western-proposed reforms now strike too close to home. They are hitting at the core of the economic-political complex that, until recently, managed Japan's phenomenal postwar economic growth. More important, outspoken Japanese frustration with Americans smacks of what psychologists call "transference," when frustration at one's own impotence in dealing with self-evident personal shortcomings is turned outward in anger at those who point out these shortcomings. In the 1980s, many Americans lashed out at the Japanese in the same way, blaming Japan for many U.S. economic problems that were clearly of America's own making.

The worst thing the United States could do, both for America's long-term self-interest and for Japan's, is to abandon *gaiatsu* in the face of Japanese protests. But *gaiatsu* can be smarter—in choosing allies within Japan, in how change is presented to Japanese society, and ultimately, in its application to Japan's real impediment to change: the political system.

In the wake of the decade-long stagnation, the postwar national consensus on the structure of the Japanese economy is showing fissures. Politicians, bureaucrats, and business leaders now all pledge fealty to reform, although they differ on the substance. Government leaders have ostensibly committed themselves to deregulation. Opinion leaders, such as economists and journalists, have emerged as new advocates of market liberalization. And a spate of scandals have challenged the authority of the main government ministries, particularly the Ministry of Finance.

The United States should actively embrace such commitments to economic deregulation and greater market access for foreigners. Wherever and whenever possible, U.S. officials should work with like-minded Japanese groups. In the 1980s, in negotiations to reform the Large-Scale Retail Store Law, American retailers were able to successfully make common cause with large-scale Japanese retailers who sought similar changes. In talks with the Japanese government to liberalize financial services, the United States worked closely behind the scenes with Japanese pension fund managers who wanted a more liberal market that would offer increased returns.

In the future, this search for allies may even mean working closely with elements of the Japanese government bureaucracy when their ambitions coincide with American goals. For example, MITI, the architect of Japan, Inc., currently touts itself as the principal advocate of deregulation within the Japanese government, albeit often deregulation of industries it does not now control. This is a transparent MITI power grab, but Washington should not be shy of working with this powerful agency if it can deliver deregulation that is meaningful for U.S. interests.

Similarly, Keidanren has increasingly come under the influence of major international corporations, such as Toyota, suggesting a power shift that could work to American advantage. As Japan's global firms face stiffer international competition, they are paying an escalating cost for Japan's failure to restructure and deregulate and could become allies in targeted efforts to change the system.

To identify potential allies and build the case for reform inside Japan, the United States should:

- *Talk softly but carry a big stick.* Public lecturing of the Japanese is increasingly counterproductive. Hollow threats undermine U.S. credibility. The better choice is to privately make American interests clear and back them with resolve.

- *Make public diplomacy in Japan a priority, targeting opinion leaders and the media.* But the United States should also take the case for restructuring and deregulation directly to the Japanese public whenever possible. In the mid-1990s, Washington lost the public relations war with Tokyo, allowing the Japanese government to paint the United States as an advocate of "managed trade," when in fact Tokyo routinely manipulated the market. More recently, the United States has identified itself with reforms—banking sector reform and deregulation—that have broad Japanese public support. Such efforts should continue. Recent cutbacks in U.S. public diplomacy in Japan must be reversed, with a new emphasis on economic and political dialogue with the Japanese conducted by a range of U.S. officials and private citizens.

* *Encourage U.S. firms in Japan to participate in the Japanese policy process, to press for better representation in Japanese industry associations, working groups, and advisory councils at the ministry level, and to get involved with government-wide deregulation policy councils where appropriate.* American companies have been quite successful with this approach in selected cases, such as discussions leading up to the January 1995 financial services agreement. With the growing U.S. corporate presence in Japan, the Japanese must afford foreigners national treatment.

* *Frame change as a deal that is too good to refuse.* Japan has always driven itself to greatness through an obsessive desire to "catch up" with the West. This seemingly inherent need to constantly measure itself against the norms of the outside world should be harnessed as an engine of change by impressing upon Tokyo the need to catch up in terms of corporate governance, providing a social safety net, and so forth. And an unsubtle message should be sent to Japan that it will *not* be treated as a member of the club of industrial nations if it continues to act like an outlier.

At the same time, it would be folly for Washington to assume that Japan is teeming with potential allies ready to sign up for a crusade to liberalize its market. Japanese consumers are suspect partners. Surveys show that price issues are still a relatively low consumer concern. And organizations such as the Japan Consumer Cooperatives Union, with its 16 million members, has conflicted interests. It is both a consumer group and a major retailer. It is partially funded by the agricultural cooperatives, and it opposed the liberalization of Japan's rice market during the Uruguay Round, despite the fact that Japanese consumers paid about seven times more than the world price.

Even many global Japanese firms are reluctant to push too hard for deregulation for fear of harming firms with which they have long-standing relationships. And the bureaucracy's near-total rejection of the reform recommendations of the government's own Economic Strategy Council indicates just how intransigent much of the bureaucracy remains.

Such limitations suggest that the United States has little choice but to continue to press for economic change in Japan—alone, if necessary, but in conjunction with a Japanese ally, if possible. But the absence of Japanese allies should never deter Washington from pursuing U.S. economic self-interest.

LAUNCH A POLITICAL DIALOGUE

The U.S.-Japan dialogue on economic reform must now broaden to include a frank discussion of the political impediments to Japan's economic renewal. This discussion will necessarily be highly sensitive, fraught with potential danger, and absolutely essential if Washington and Tokyo are to get at the real issues threatening their economic relationship in the long term.

A more democratic Japanese political system is a necessary precursor to a more market-oriented Japanese economy. "Japan's failure to act [on a range of economic issues] seems to boil down to a simple lack of political courage," former investment banker R. Taggart Murphy has written. That failure of political will reflects the fact that, as economic journalist Richard Katz has written, "The very features of Japan's economy that hobble growth are also the pillars of its politics."

Japan's postwar political and economic system bound together the internationally competitive and the domestic, inefficient sectors of Japan's economy in a symbiotic relationship with the political elite. Elected officials and the bureaucracy gave business access to credit and protected it from foreign competition in return for political support. For decades, this Faustian bargain proved tremendously successful both at spurring economic growth and at entrenching bureaucracy and the Liberal Democratic Party. Bureaucrats favored industries and were rewarded with lucrative jobs upon retirement. Electoral laws gave disproportionate political strength to rural areas, and politicians responded by protecting farmers and construction interests at the expense of urban consumers and more productive industries. Money politics gave untoward influence to big corporations and party bosses.

Japan's prolonged economic stagnation has called into question the future sustainability of these arrangements. Conflicting interests have, on occasion, led to bureaucratic and political gridlock, such as the dangerous delay in dealing with the huge debts hanging over the banking system. The construction industry's political influence continues to distort public works spending, dissipating its stimulative impact. As long as rural voters have several times the electoral influence of urban voters, as long as campaign donations are allowed to play such a major role in Japanese electoral politics, as long as members of the Japanese Diet are dependent on bureaucrats to craft legislative proposals, America's economic problems with Japan will persist.

For this reason, the United States should:

- *Treat Japan's political system as a structural impediment to economic liberalization.* An official bilateral dialogue on this topic would strike too close to the nerve of national sovereignty. But Washington and Tokyo could sanction an informal dialogue—a two-track approach between academics, political leaders, and former government officials—to air differing perspectives and craft recommendations for political change. Such an interchange would necessarily be mutual, because the United States itself has an eighteenth century political system that impedes twenty-first century economics. For example, such an exchange could focus on the U.S. experience in adapting to a one-person, one-vote electoral system or on the corrosive influence and the high cost of money politics in both economies.

- *Tailor trade, deregulation, and other reform initiatives with Japan toward issues of concern to urban Japanese constituencies.* Such a focus would help surface Japanese allies for American concerns. More important, it would leverage the ruling Liberal Democratic Party, whose power remains rooted in rural areas, to accept change or risk losing the urban votes it increasingly needs to stay in power.

CREATING A U.S.–JAPAN OPEN MARKET PLACE BY 2010

A strengthened U.S. emphasis on macroeconomic questions and a more aggressive posture on individual trade disputes are necessary but not sufficient initiatives to recast the U.S.-Japan economic relationship. Taken in isolation, such efforts will fail to address the long-term, systemic trends in the relationship and the structural problems hampering further transpacific economic integration. Moreover, they will risk being characterized as little more than Japan-bashing. Finally, it took the United States an entire decade to restructure its economy. Japan may face an even more time-consuming challenge. The U.S.-Japan relationship needs greater coherence to withstand this difficult period of adjustment.

At the same time, the United States demands a greater, faster restructuring of the Japanese economy, the resolution of long-standing bilateral trade problems, and meaningful Japanese leadership at the multilateral level. So, Washington should also propose negotiations to create an open marketplace between itself and Tokyo by the year 2010.

Such an initiative would address deregulation in Japan, the enforcement of competition policy, distribution questions, land-use restrictions, foreign investment, and the importation of manufactured products, among other things. This more ambitious grandson of SII would be reciprocal. The United States would have to address some of its own market impediments, such as the low American savings rate, government procurement practices, its patent system, and individual tariffs and quantitative restrictions on imports.

Creating a U.S.-Japan open marketplace would be a bold undertaking. For a new president, a new Congress, and a new Japanese government, it would provide an opportunity to set off bilateral relations in a new direction in the new millennium. For Washington it would provide the opportunity to show creative new international leadership, reaffirm U.S. commitment to trade and investment liberalization, and stabilize relations with its most important Asian ally by establishing a framework for dealing with future economic problems. For Tokyo, the pledge to create an open marketplace would reaffirm Japan's ongoing commitment to structural economic reform and deregulation, dispelling lingering doubts among global investors while demonstrating that Japan is capable of bold initiatives. Moreover, for the United States such an effort would provide the carrot in U.S.-Japan economic relations to compliment the already recommended stick of greater assertiveness to insure that U.S. economic policy toward Japan is balanced and two-tracked.

The 2010 open marketplace initiative would require the following:

- a feasibility study, to be completed by the end of 2001;

- the launch of the initiative by early 2002;

- the creation of a U.S.-Japan business dialogue to identify market barriers and the establishment of parallel legislative and regulatory dialogues to support the process;

- an early harvest of meaningful benefits—deregulation in Japan, increased FDI, and increased manufactured imports—to demonstrate the credibility of the effort;

- an annual summit between the American president and the Japanese prime minister to drive the negotiating process;

- parallel negotiations with Australia, the EU, New Zealand, and Singapore to demonstrate to Japan that the United States still pursue its economic self-interest in all possible forums;

- the test of success for this initiative would be a reduction in the current bilateral imbalance of trade and investment and a growth of U.S.-Japan economic interaction over time.

It took Europe from 1957 to 1992 to create a single market. And the slow pace of implementation by the member states of the European Community's single market directives demonstrates just how difficult economic integration can be. But the European Union would not be where it is today—arguably far more integrated than anyone ever thought possible a decade ago—if it had not begun to move in the direction of a single market more than a generation ago.

A U.S.-Japan open marketplace is not as ambitious as Europe's single market. The goal would not be to create a single currency or to build a central bureaucracy comparable to the European Commission. Moreover, the United States and Japan will almost certainly not fully integrate their economies within a decade, even if that objective became the top priority of both governments (which it most certainly will not). But if Washington and Tokyo make an open marketplace a conscious bilateral goal, they will achieve far more economic integration than they would if they simply let history take its course or merely focused on immediate bilateral trade frictions. Admittedly, this will require a leap of faith in an economic relationship long beset by turmoil. But without a vision of where they are headed, the United States and Japan risk being lost in the maze of day-to-day problems.

NOT A NEW IDEA

A proposal for deeper integration of the American and Japanese economies is not new. The president's 1997 Commission on United States–Pacific Trade and Investment Policy recommended that the United States negotiate a "Comprehensive Market Agreement" with Japan that "would include all the aspects of a standard free trade agreement, but would go beyond such a pact by creating agreed upon procedures with regard to investment, anticompetitive business practices, administrative procedures, and a range of other sectoral matters often identified as structural trade and investment barriers."

Nor is it novel to pursue a dual track in economic relations with Japan: a tough, pragmatic, issue-oriented approach in the short run, combined with a long-term effort to cooperatively reduce structural impediments to commercial ties.

Just such a policy was announced in May 1989, when then-USTR Carla Hills targeted Japan under the new Super 301 legislation designed to deal with technical barriers to trade and discriminatory public procurement practices. At the same time, she proposed launching the SII. The goals of this dual approach were to demonstrate to Congress and the Japanese that the Bush administration could be tough on trade issues, but also to suggest to Tokyo that aggressive unilateralism was only one aspect of U.S. policy toward Japan and that Washington was willing to more broadly negotiate greater market access over time. There are tactical and strategic reasons to again pursue such a carrot and stick approach.

The USTR must constantly balance the substantive merit of individual trade cases against Japan with the political pressure individual industries can place on the USTR to take up their cause. All too often, these cases must be weighed one at a time, without much regard for the broader sweep of U.S.-Japan relations.

Through the articulation of a long-term market integration initiative, individual trade disputes can be put in some context. Rather than dealing with issues seriatim, the USTR can better pick and choose its fights without having to reject individual grievances out of hand. Strong unfair trade cases of immediate importance can be dealt with as they are now—either bilaterally or through a WTO dispute settlement case. Other petitions can be raised as part of the open marketplace negotiation, with the option always remaining to address the issue more directly in the future.

This is a time-tested tactic that would give the USTR added flexibility in dealing with Japan. In the 1980s, for example, the U.S. Rice Millers Association brought a Section 301 case to the USTR aimed at dismantling Japanese import barriers. Then-USTR Clayton Yeutter, knowing full well that the Rice Millers' had a very good case but realizing that such aggressive unilateralism could destroy the Uruguay Round of multilateral trade negotiations then in progress, deflected their petition by convincing the plaintiffs that he could address their concerns in the broader multilateral negotiation. Future USTRs need similar discretion to pick and choose their battles with Japan, but they will not always have the alternative of a multilateral negotiation.

A two-track approach with Japan will also create more maneuvering room for Japanese politicians and bureaucrats under pressure not to fold to American demands. By lowering the visibility of a trade dispute by subsuming it in the open marketplace initiative, Japanese negotiators may have greater flexibility to make progress.

Finally, issue-by-issue trade negotiating tends to be driven by specific corporate complaints and is thus episodic, reactive, and adversarial. It casts the United States as a bully while enabling Japanese negotiators to assume the position of defender of the national patrimony against unreasonable foreign demands. The result is an increasingly embittered and distrustful U.S.-Japan relationship. A comprehensive negotiation casts the relationship in a broader perspective.

An umbrella-like framework for U.S.-Japan economic relations also affords other important strategic benefits. It reassures the world that individual trade disputes between Washington and Tokyo are only torn threads in a richer fabric and will not rend the broader relationship. It is a clear signal to Japan that the United States wants a mature economic relationship, one in which both governments can fight tooth and nail over discreet issues without fear because they are both broadly committed to closer economic ties over time. It will also signal to Wall Street that every trade fight with Japan is not a precursor to a trade war. And it will help curb the Pentagon's and the State Department's meddling, curbing their tendency to second guess the USTR's handling of trade disputes by making it official U.S. policy that individual disputes will not jeopardize the broader relationship.

SETTING A GOAL

An open-ended commitment by Washington and Tokyo to closer economic ties at some point in the distant future would have little public credibility and no bureaucratic impetus. An open marketplace initiative needs to be a time specific endeavor, with a goal that is not too close, so as to be unrealistic, and not so far into the future as to be irrelevant.

A New Beginning

The Japanese and American governments are already party to such a commitment, the pledge made by the member nations of the Asia Pacific Economic Cooperation forum at the 1994 APEC meeting in Bogor, Indonesia to achieve free trade among the industrial nations of the region by the year 2010. This goal involves Australia, Singapore, and New Zealand, as well as Japan and the United States. But, realistically, with the United States being the largest economy in the world and Japan accounting for the lion's share of all economic activity in Asia, the objective is only attainable if Washington and Tokyo lead the way.

The decade-long time frame is the appropriate context, long enough to allow markets to achieve much of the objective on their own and short enough to lend some urgency to the work of the negotiators.

But, despite the wording of the APEC commitment, simply a free trade area among the major industrial nations of the region is not the appropriate goal. Trade-weighted tariffs are already low in the Asia Pacific and headed lower. Simply eliminating tariff peaks would do little to accelerate economic integration. Truly free trade in the region can only be achieved through the systematic elimination of nontariff barriers to trade and investment: discriminatory domestic regulatory regimes, government practices that discriminate against foreign competitors and so forth. It is for this reason that Tokyo and Washington should set their own, more ambitious goal of creating an open marketplace by 2010.

A NEED FOR BALANCE

The weight of adjustment in creating an open marketplace will undoubtedly fall most heavily on Japan. Starting with one market—America's—that is among the most open in the world and a market—Japan's—that is the most closed among major industrial nations, meaningful integration will never be achieved in a relevant time frame through tit-for-tat deregulation and liberalization. The onus of change will initially and primarily be on Tokyo.

This does not mean, however, that there are not market barriers in the United States or that American adjustment to an open marketplace will be painless. For both substantive and political reasons, a market-integration dialogue can not and should not be a monologue. Tokyo will have its own macroeconomic and bilateral trade and investment issues to raise with Washington and the United States should take them seriously, because they will be in America's self-interest.

On the macroeconomic level, despite the recent elimination of the federal budget deficit, the low level of personal savings in the United States is one of the main reasons the overall national savings rate in America remains relatively low, which, in turn, accounts for the persistent U.S. current account deficit. From a Japanese perspective, tensions over the bilateral trade balance will continue as long as the United States consumes so much more than it saves. Just as in the late 1980s, when Tokyo suggested that Washington curb its budget deficit, the Japanese will be likely to pressure Americans to save more to curtail its consumption of world capital.

This is a legitimate issue for the Japanese to raise, because it is a source of bilateral friction, because with its aging population Japan will not be able to supply the United States with as much capital as it did in the past and because emerging markets will increasing compete for the capital now flowing to the United States to service its debt. Moreover, this is a problem that the United States itself needs to solve to curb the burgeoning indebtedness of the American economy and the economic vulnerabilities that creates. The solutions that Tokyo may suggest—such as using the current federal budget surplus to reduce the national debt and thus further raise national savings, rather than spend it through tax cuts or new government expenditures—may not be politically palatable in some quarters in the United States. But they are reasonable suggestions to be raised by America's new partner in economic integration.

More specifically on the trade front, stung by their recent treatment in the steel antidumping cases the Japanese are likely to want to discuss American application of U.S. antidumping legislation, including the finding of dumping in almost all cases and the lack of "appropriate" adjustment of dumping margins for exchange rate fluctuations. In the current U.S. political environment, such issues would appear to be off the table. But cast in a broader context, as an issue to be taken up once there is meaningful enforcement of Japanese antitrust laws, it is a discussion the United States must be willing to have if it expects Japan to have similar dialogues on other politically "untouchable" issues.

Tokyo will also want to raise other trade concerns. Some U.S. tariffs remain high, such as the 25 percent duty on imported trucks. The U.S. "first-to-invent" patent principle is at odds with the "first-to-file" principle used in Japan and much of the rest of the world, complicating technological cooperation. "Buy America" legislation favoring domestic suppliers in road building, mass transit and rail transportation discriminates against foreign suppliers. This is a particular problem at the state and local level, where half of all government procurement takes place.

By comparison with the U.S. laundry list of concerns, Japan's complaints are relatively limited. But they are no less politically charged and, at least at first blush, no less intractable than many of America's concerns about the functioning of the Japanese market. During the SII talks, Japan had its own agenda for change in America. But Tokyo was timid in raising those issues and Washington was dismissive in considering them. Nevertheless, many of Japan's concerns have been addressed by the United States, including reforming American management techniques and improving the competitiveness of U.S. industry. If an "open-marketplace" dialogue is to have any semblance of balance and have any chance of political acceptance in Japan, Tokyo must be more assertive in proffering advice and Washington must be more receptive to that counsel.

A BLUEPRINT

Such an ambitious goal cannot be reached without a road map, with markers along the way to measure progress and a minimum speed limit to insure the objective is reached in the agreed upon timeframe.

The political credibility of an open marketplace initiative will be dependent upon a fairly specific negotiating agenda and timetable. For a skeptical American public and business community, an early harvest of negotiating achievements will be necessary to build confidence that this is a serious exercise intent on delivering meaningful, timely results.

The content of such negotiations and their objectives would be set by mutual agreement, would be phased and layered to build upon one another and would be subject to change as economic conditions evolved. The topics for negotiation would include, but certainly not be limited to: domestic regulation of everything from pharmaceuticals to accounting to retail distribution, competition policy, tax policy, investment, government procurement, accreditation of professionals, technical standards, and testing and so forth.

The goal would be mutual recognition of regulations where appropriate, harmonization of regulation where possible, deregulation where feasible, and pro-competitive regulation where necessary. The test of success would be the reduction of the current imbalance in trade and investment and greater economic interchange over time.

Washington and Tokyo may also want to lift a page from the European experience and establish mutual macroeconomic objectives as a means of helping to force microeconomic adjustment.

In the end, creation of a U.S.-Japan open marketplace by a date certain will not be as important as the process both Tokyo and Washington have engaged in to get there. A blueprint for building a house is a plan that may or may not ever be realized. The problems the contractor encounters, the delays and compromises the builder must make almost invariably alter the vision of the architect. But a home is still habitable, even if the attic or basement is unfinished by the closing date. And the carpenter's shortcomings do not invalidate the blueprint.

A New Beginning

SUPPORTING INSTITUTIONS

A U.S.-Japan open marketplace initiative can only succeed if it is part of a concerted effort by both business and government to institutionalize the process of integration.

The principal driving force behind the creation of a transatlantic marketplace is the Transatlantic Business Dialogue (TABD), comprised of more than 130 European and American CEOs of major and minor companies. The Dialogue is broken down into working groups addressing issues of standards and regulatory policy such as mutual recognition agreements, electronic commerce, global issues such as services and intellectual property, business facilitation such as customs procedures and taxation, and the concerns of small and medium-sized companies. Company staffs from both sides of the Atlantic meet regularly among themselves and with government officials to hammer out an action agenda. And once a year the CEOs meet to bless the products of the working groups, to chart a course for the subsequent year and, most important, to convey to top government officials the imperative they place on resolution of the market impediments that they have jointly identified.

A similar U.S.-Japan Business Dialogue would be a necessary complement of an open marketplace initiative. Corporations are interested in practical, timely benefits of economic liberalization. And only the bilateral business community can identify significant barriers to trade, investment and commercial operations in Japan, prioritize them, suggest what might be done to eliminate or minimize them and mobilize the political will to make that happen. Past efforts at a U.S.-Japan business dialogue have failed because they have been dominated by American firms more interested in preserving their niche in the Japanese market than in broadening trade and investment and because Japanese participants have refused to deviate from their government's talking points. To be successful, a business dialogue must include a wide range of firms, American companies with close Japanese ties and those hoping to break into the Japan market and upstart Japanese firms willing to speak their own mind.

Of course, the stakeholders in a U.S.-Japan open marketplace extend beyond the business community to include organized labor, consumers and environmentalists among others. There are transatlantic dialogues between all of these groups and there should be similar discussions, where feasible, as part of a U.S.-Japan initiative. They would add breadth and depth to the market integration effort. And, realistically, these groups could assert a political veto over the enterprise if it ignored workers' interests, threatened health and safety or harmed the environment.

A seminal lesson from the first years of the TABD was the lack of commitment by the U.S. Food and Drug administration, the Environmental Protection Agency and similar domestic regulatory entities on both sides of the Atlantic. In their defense, trade and foreign market integration have never been a priority for these bodies. And they are accountable to domestically oriented legislative committees, not the committees traditionally involved with trade concerns. It is little wonder then that initially they were obstacles to, rather then facilitators of, progress. To overcome that roadblock a transatlantic regulatory dialogue has begun.

A similar dialogue would be essential between the United States and Japan. The antitrust division of the U.S. Justice Department already confers regularly with the Japan Fair Trade Commission and other agencies have limited exchange programs. But a formal regulatory dialogue would have a much more focused purpose: mutual recognition of pharmaceutical approvals, the streamlining of patent filing procedures and so forth.

To drive the open marketplace initiative, key players at the sub-cabinet level in both the Japanese and U.S. governments—from the vice-minister of Japan's Ministry of International Trade and Industry to the undersecretaries at the U.S. Department of Agriculture—should meet on a regular basis. The Japanese government has long pushed for such regular sub-cabinet level gatherings. The U.S. government has resisted, justifiably worried that this emphasis on process rather than concrete results would lead the meetings to be little more than talking shops. But a new joint undertaking would provide such meetings with a purpose and a deadline, focusing their work.

In the past, coordination of U.S. initiatives toward Japan has often been frustrated by interagency turf fights, with the State or Defense Departments reigning in USTR or the Treasury overruling the Commerce Department. And continuity of policy toward Japan has been a recurrent problem, both in the transition between administrations or even within the term of a single administration (such as the abrupt down shifting of the Clinton administration's aggressive posture toward Japan from mid-1995 onward).

Some such discontinuity is inescapable as priorities adjust to changing conditions and elections bring new actors and ideas into play. But the value of a long-term commitment to create an U.S.-Japan open marketplace is that such an overarching goal is flexible enough to transcend year-to-year or administration-to-administration nuances in approaches to Japan and to provide much-needed and long-neglected continuity in the economic relationship.

Nevertheless, there will still be a need, inside the U.S. government at least, for one bureaucratic actor to have the responsibility and authority to drive the open marketplace process and to be accountable if it stumbles. That duty might best be vested in the deputy director of the National Economic Council (NEC) or that person's equivalent at the National Security Council (NSC). Whatever this person's title, it is crucial that he or she sit in the White House. Only someone with a broad international and domestic regulatory mandate will have the breadth of understanding and, more important, the political clout to force progress on a range of market integration issues. USTR, the Commerce, and Treasury Departments all have their own agendas and are not trusted by their counterparts to be neutral brokers. The NEC and the NSC were created to play such a role.

A business dialogue, and sub-cabinet level meetings are pointillist by nature. They will tend to focus on the trees not the forest. The harmonization of headlight standards and similar mundane agenda items that will arise in the process of creating an open marketplace are building bloc activities. While commercially or socially beneficial, they will, by their nature, tend to bog down over time. Sole focus on these issues will insure that market integration is never accomplished in a relevant time frame. That can only be achieved through the vision and impetus provided by the active engagement of political leadership.

To that end, members of the U.S. Congress and the Japanese Diet should meet regularly to assess progress toward an open marketplace. These gatherings would differ substantively from current parliamentary exchanges because they would be an integral monitoring process of an ongoing bilateral negotiation. Diet members and members of Congress would hold negotiators feet to the fire, work to eliminate bottlenecks and come to a mutual understanding of differences that are irreconcilable. To be successful, the legislative dialogue would require the participation of the chairmen and subcommittee chairmen of legislative committees with domestic regulatory responsibilities. Only they, not members of the Senate Foreign Relations Committee or similar Diet Committees have the interest in the pharmaceutical approval process or the auto safety implications of seat belt positioning, the nuts and bolts issues that will be the mortar of a U.S.-Japan marketplace. And only these elected officials, with their power of the purse, have the leverage over domestic regulators to insure that the bureaucrats will take this effort seriously.

Clearly, such a dialogue is likely to suffer from the relative lack of power and influence of individual members of the Japanese Diet, another manifestation of the defects of Japan's political system. That shortcoming cannot be rectified over night. But delaying the dialogue until the Diet is a more independent player holds an open marketplace hostage in a chicken and egg debate. The very act of engaging Diet members in substantive exchanges may be of help in strengthening their roles in the Japanese political system.

Of course, nothing captures the imagination of a nation, focuses the attention of bureaucrats, and signals intent to the business community like the involvement of government leaders. For that reason, the U.S. president and the Japanese prime minister should meet in an annual summit to review progress toward an open marketplace. Leaders are loath to meet without something to announce. So this action-forcing event may do more than anything else to push along market integration. The yearly meeting will also pro-

vide an opportunity to review progress on a range of diplomatic
and security issues. If the president can find the time and the ratio-
nale to meet every six months with the president of the European
Union, it is certainly worth his effort to meet regularly with the
prime minister of the world's other major economic power in a dialogue that is more substantive than a photo-op on the fringes of
the G-7 or APEC meetings.

EXPLOIT LEVERAGE

Even the most compelling and timely of ideas rarely succeed
simply on their own merits. Progress is often dependent upon external pressures and the relationship of one set of goals to a broader galaxy of national objectives and bilateral concerns. Moreover,
only the leveraging of other goals and initiatives is likely to convince Tokyo that Washington is serious about fundamentally
changing and improving America's economic relationship with Japan.

An open marketplace exercise would not and could not stand
alone. It should be seen as another thread in the ever-tightening
texture of U.S.-Japan relations. The initiative would parallel the
evolution of the U.S.-Japan security relationship, in which Japan
is slowly taking on greater responsibilities for its own defense and
for the security of the region through its signing of the Defense
Guidelines, participation in theater missile defense (TMD) and
the contribution of Japanese forces to multilateral peace keeping
operations. Although for diplomatic reasons the U.S.-Japan security and economic relationships are likely to remain on separate
tracks, politically they can never be fully divorced. Once Tokyo and
Washington embark on the path toward the creation of an open
marketplace, it must be made clear to the Japanese that failure to
demonstrate progress in that direction will inevitably heighten bilateral trade frictions that will inexorably undermine American public support for the U.S.-Japan security relationship.

To counter expected Japanese reluctance to enter into an open
marketplace negotiation and to make it clear to Tokyo that there
will be a price for failure to take the exercise seriously, the United

States should simultaneously launch parallel initiatives with Australia, New Zealand, Singapore, and Korea. All of these nations are similarly committed to the 2010 deadline and one or more may be quite willing to seize such an opportunity, whether or not Japan is so inclined. Of course, if all agree, realization of the 2010 goal might actually be within reach.

At the same time, the United States should intensify its efforts at integration of the European and Western Hemisphere economies. The Japanese business community and government is made exceedingly nervous by any indication that the United States and the European Union may be stealing a jump on them, intent on establishing a global technological standard or a consensus on commercial rules of the road without Japanese input. The United States should fully exploit this anxiety by making it clear to Tokyo that America intends to pursue its self-interest in a variety of forums and that Japan can join in that enterprise or be left by the roadside. This posture will hopefully spark greater Japanese interest in bilateral economic integration efforts.

Japan is not devoid of such leverage itself and can be expected to pursue it. Tokyo has already entered into preliminary discussions about the creation of free trade areas with South Korea, Singapore and Mexico. Such initiatives, and MITI's call for regional free trade agreements in its year 2000 policy white paper, are signs of Japan's new-found willingness to engage in bilateral market integration and its capacity to move in this direction on its own if Washington chooses not to pursue a U.S.-Japan open marketplace.

<h2 style="text-align:center">A VISION TEMPERED BY EXPERIENCE</h2>

Ambition and vision can be naive and counterproductive if they are not tempered by experience. There is no disputing that the case for a U.S.-Japan open marketplace rests more on the needs for the future than on the track record of the past.

The political climate for a U.S.-Japan economic integration initiative is not good. The bitter legacy of the 1980s—when Japanese imports and investments were blamed by many Americans for the destruction of the domestic American consumer electronics industry, the dismantling of the steel industry and the severe down sizing of the auto industry—still poisons many American attitudes toward Japan. Similarly, Japanese frustration with American *gaiatsu* during much of the 1990s has never been higher.

The confrontation over Japanese steel shipments to the United States and the rising U.S. trade deficit with Japan are high profile, immediate bilateral problems that threaten to crowd out any serious discussion of long-term economic initiatives. Politically, Japanese progress in resolving proximate issues will be a necessary prerequisite for any American administration's ability to undertake a more positive agenda and Congress' willingness to support it.

At the same time, a toning down of public U.S. criticism of Japan and an American willingness to publicly praise Japanese economic initiatives where appropriate will be politically necessary for any Japanese government to embrace deeper cooperation with the United States.

Yet both Washington and Tokyo must be careful not to let their mutual, long-run self-interest be totally held hostage by day-to-day trade frictions, however important they may be. In fact, one value of pursuing a long-term objective is to help put those tensions in some perspective. In 1999, there was no threat that the high-profile American fight with the European Union over bananas would sabotage the ongoing transatlantic economic dialogue. Brussels and Washington were able to have two-track discussions on economics. This lesson is instructive. If two economic super powers do not have a long-term goal defining their economic relationship, that relationship gets defined by a laundry list of short-term problems. This is the trap Washington and Tokyo now find themselves in. An open marketplace initiative is the way out.

Unfortunately, the obstacles to economic integration are even more profound than current bilateral trade problems, such as steel or flat glass. They are deeply rooted at the intersection of culture and self-interest. There are great differences between Japan and the United States in economic and business philosophy.

There is no common understanding of the role of the state in the economy, of the proper relationship between supposedly competing firms or of the "proper" balance of interests between various economic stake holders: workers, consumers, members of the community and the owners of capital.

Such differences are far greater between Japan and America than they are between France and Germany or between the United States and Europe. And the level of economic integration—whether measured by FDI or two-way trade—is less. And yet even the European integration effort and the attempts to craft a transatlantic marketplace have been forced to move at a snail's pace because of these disparities.

Skeptics justifiably question whether it is possible to achieve a meaningful integration of two economies with such differences. History suggests not. Recent business developments—mounting foreign investment in Japan, the transformation of American management along Japanese lines—suggest that once unimaginable things are now possible.

But the question facing both Washington and Tokyo is not whether such differences in perspective and goals exist, but what can or should be done in a public policy sense in the face of them.

In the 1980s, revisionist analysts of Japan argued that transpacific disparities were so great that Japan could never and would never adopt Western or global standards, They contended that the only way to accommodate Japan's growing economic weight in the world was to deal with it at arm's length, to negotiate numerical targets for imports and foreign investment. Subsequent experience suggested that, while revisionists overestimated Japan's long-term economic trajectory, they understood the intractability of Japanese business and political culture in the short run.

Yet, experience over the last decade demonstrates that any such conscious walling off of Japan—as analytically appealing as it might be—is just not a viable option both for diplomatic and security reasons and because the size of the Japanese economy and U.S. reliance on Japanese capital does not afford America that luxury.

Of course, there are profound, practical obstacles to integrating the Japanese and American markets. Any such initiative would necessarily involve a rapid acceleration of the deregulation of the Japanese economy. As noted earlier, Tokyo's track record on deregulation in general, and in its recent deregulation talks with the United States in particular, is mixed at best. And there is always the chance that Tokyo could use the launching of a ten-year open marketplace process as an excuse to further postpone politically difficult economic restructuring. Any market-opening initiative would have to credibly confront this issue head on, with demonstrations of Japan's good faith through an acceleration of deregulation.

The success of any economic integration effort would be critically dependent upon the enthusiastic engagement of both the American and Japanese business communities. It was the demands of European corporations that forced the pace of European integration and similar expectations will be necessary in the United States and Japan. The American business community, especially that in Tokyo, is profoundly skeptical of any effort at ambitious, comprehensive market integration negotiations with Japan. In their experience only issue-by-issue market liberalizing efforts deliver results. And any broad-based, long-term effort would unavoidably dilute the governmental and business community resources needed to achieve those ends. At the same time, U.S. business interests in Japan are changing, as American investment in Japan grows. The new American actors inside the Japanese market have a growing interest in the transparency of Japanese government actions, the enforcement of competition policy and open public procurement. These are all issues that can best be addressed in an open marketplace negotiation.

More narrowly, the Japanese business community is divided on the desirability and the feasibility of even a limited U.S.-Japan business dialogue. The U.S.-Japan Business Council, the foremost bilateral meeting of business leaders from both nations, has proved to be of limited usefulness. And recent efforts to use this group as the basis of a U.S.-Japan business dialogue reflect neither a desire to replicate the detailed, proactive nature of the Transatlantic

Business Dialogue, nor any interest in overcoming the TABD's own limitations.

Yet such business community opposition should not be unexpected. The reaction of European and American corporations to the Clinton administration's first proposals for a TABD ranged from skeptical to hostile. It took political leadership to get business to come around to the idea. And a U.S.-Japan business dialogue is not likely to get off the ground without a similar push from Tokyo and Washington.

Of course, the TABD itself has fallen far short of expectations. When it was launched, it was hoped that the process might produce a half-dozen mutual recognition agreements a year. Yet after four years it had only a half dozen to show for its efforts. A U.S.-Japan Business Dialogue would have to be designed so that it could deliver more tangible results earlier, possibly as a result of the regulatory dialogue proposed above and more overt political expectations. Given the skepticism about a U.S.-Japan initiative, such an early harvest would be critical.

Another objection to an open marketplace initiative is that neither Washington nor Tokyo take the APEC 2010 goal seriously. Neither government has made a conscious effort to assess what changes would be necessary in its domestic practices or in the practices of its counterpart to enable the target to be met. So 2010 is a false objective.

More important, Japan's recent track record in APEC does not give much reason for optimism. Tokyo's refusal in late 1998 to eliminate or substantially reduce tariffs for fish and forest products sabotaged APEC's Early Voluntary Sectoral Liberalization initiative in nine sectors involving trade totaling $1.5 trillion dollars.

A more difficult problem may arise from Japanese unwillingness to engage in any market integration effort under the continued "threat" of U.S. trade actions. This will be the acid test of Tokyo's willingness, or lack of willingness, to improve the bilateral economic relationship over time. It must be made clear to Tokyo that this is not an "either-or" proposition. The aggressive U.S. pursuit of its economic self-interest will continue both bilaterally and through the WTO. That is a given. Japan can work to mitigate these bilateral frictions through a comprehensive negotiation intent on changing the overall context of the relationship. Or it can fight a series of rear guard actions that threaten to get increasingly ugly. But it can not avoid dealing with the impediments that deny foreigners access to its market or impede foreign investors' realizing the fruits of their investments.

Finally, trade theologians will undoubtedly argue that any effort to accelerate U.S.-Japan economic integration is a manifestation of insidious regionalism and will undercut the next round of multilateral trade negotiations. Concerns about opportunity costs are real given the limited resources available to the USTR and the limited amount of time and political energy any president or prime minister is likely to be willing to devote to this goal.

But the creation of the European Community in 1957 did not fatally undermine the Dillon Round or the Kennedy Round of international trade talks. The creation of the single European market in 1992 did not sabotage the Uruguay Round. And, despite trade theory, the experience of both the North American Free Trade Agreement and the APEC suggests that, rather than impeding progress, such regional efforts spurred completion of the Uruguay Round.

The resource allocation issue is one the U.S. government simply has to address head on. While there are ways to reallocate personnel and find new pots of money for some activities, in the end the next administration and Congress have to decide if economic relations with the world's second-largest economy are worth the investment.

A PRAGMATIC APPROACH

U.S.-Japan economic integration is increasing and ever deeper integration seems inevitable. The challenge for the United States is how best to deal with Japan's profound reluctance to change. Issue-by-issue negotiations afford the advantage of not raising unrealistic expectations of what can and cannot be accomplished. But they are unlikely to push the envelope of change Japan may be capable of accomplishing. An open marketplace initiative risks foundering on impractical goals, but it does create a process within which Japan can be encouraged to change as much as it is able and willing.

Faced with this conundrum, there may be no way to find common ground between the American and Japanese economies. Yet the only way to know that for sure is to try, to enter into an economic integration effort with limited, hardheaded expectations and hope to be pleasantly surprised.

To that end, the U.S. government should not jump headlong into a market integration effort with Japan. The new U.S. president, with the advice of the new Congress should propose to Tokyo a one-year feasibility study for an open marketplace initiative. This study could lay out the goals of such an exercise and the methods and negotiating modalities for achieving those goals in a systematic fashion. If the recommendation is to proceed, actual negotiations could begin in 2002.

CONCLUSION

The U.S.-Japan economic relationship is of pivotal importance to the global economy. If it fosters mutual growth and interdependence, the American and Japanese people and those of the world will benefit immeasurably. If domestic preoccupations and bilateral tensions dominate the relationship, the world will be a poorer place.

Markets will ultimately determine the individual success or failure of the American and Japanese economies and of their joint interaction. But governments will shape that environment and influence its outcome.

A new U.S. president, a new American Congress, and a new Japanese government have a unique opportunity at the beginning of a new decade to chart a fresh course for U.S.-Japan economic relations. It is a chance not afforded many leaders and an occasion not to be lightly foregone. It will require political risk-taking, diplomatic tough mindedness, business acumen, and statesmanlike vision. The world's two largest economies and those around the globe who depend upon them deserve no less.

MEMBERS OF THE STUDY GROUP

WILLIAM ARCHEY, American Electronics Association

C. FRED BERGSTEN, Institute for International Economics

JEFF BINGAMAN, U.S. Senate (D–N. Mex.)

STEVEN C. CLEMONS, New America Foundation

W. BOWMAN CUTTER, E.M. Warburg, Pincus & Co., LLC

ERIC GANGLOFF, Japan-U.S. Friendship Commission

MICHAEL GREEN, Council on Foreign Relations

AMO HOUGHTON, U.S. House of Representatives (R–N.Y.)

MERIT JANOW, Columbia University

CHARLES D. LAKE II, AFLAC Japan

TAMERA S. LUZZATTO, Office of Senator Rockefeller

EDWARD LINCOLN, The Brookings Institution

HARALD MALMGREN, Malmgren Group

PHILIPPA MALMGREN, Warburg, Dillon, Read

ROBERT A. MANNING, Council on Foreign Relations

RICHARD MEDLEY, Medley Global Advisors

Editors Note: Members participated as individuals and not in their institutional capacity. Affiliation, as of the date of publication, is for information purposes only. The views expressed in this book are solely the author's and do not necessarily reflect those of any study group member.

[108]

A New Beginning

MARGARET MIHORI, Japan-U.S. Friendship Commission

MARCUS NOLAND, Institute for International Economics

GEORGE R. PACKARD, U.S.-Japan Foundation

CLYDE V. PRESTOWITZ JR., Economic Strategy Institute

TIM REGAN, Corning, Inc.

RICHARD RIVERS, Attorney

JAY ROCKEFELLER, U.S. Senate (D–W. Va.)

SHERMAN ROBINSON, International Food Policy Research Institute

THOMAS C. SAWYER, U.S. House of Representatives, (D–Ohio)

LEONARD SCHOPPA, University of Virgina

IRA SHAPIRO, Long, Aldridge & Norman

JAMES J. SHINN, Princeton University

MICHAEL B. SMITH, Global USA, Inc.

RANDALL SODERQUIST, Office of Senator Bingaman

JIM SOUTHWICK, Dorsey & Whitney

BRUCE STOKES, Council on Foreign Relations

DANIEL TARULLO, Georgetown University Law Center

MARK TILTON, Purdue University

ROBERT VAN WICKLIN, Office of Representative Houghton

STEVEN VOGEL, University of California, Berkeley

ALAN WOLFF, Dewey Ballantine LLP

IRA WOLF, Office of Senator Max Baucus

BIBLIOGRAPHY

A number of excellent books have been published in recent years on U.S.-Japan economic relations that helped shape the author's thinking on Japan and guided the study group's discussions. They include:

Leonard J. Schoppa, *Bargaining With Japan* (New York: Columbia University Press, 1997).

Lonny E. Carlile and Mark C. Tilton, editors, *Is Japan Really Changing?* (Washington, D.C.: The Brookings Institution, 1998).

Patrick Smith, *Japan: A Reinterpretation* (New York: Vintage Books, 1998).

Richard Katz, *Japan: The System That Soured* (Armonk, N.Y.: M.E. Sharpe, 1998).

Adam S. Posen, *Restoring Japan's Economic Growth* (Washington, D.C.: Institute for International Economics, 1998).

Gerald L. Curtis, *The Logic of Japanese Politics* (New York: Columbia University Press, 1999).

Edward J. Lincoln, *Troubled Times* (Washington, D.C.: Brookings Institution, 1999).

9 7 8 0 8 7 6 0 9 2 7 3 6